SILICON GOLD RUSH

THE NEXT GENERATION
OF HIGH–TECH STARS
REWRITES THE RULES OF BUSINESS

KAREN SOUTHWICK, Upside Magazine

John Wiley & Sons, Inc.

New York • Chichester • Weinheim • Brisbane • Singapore • Toronto

This book is printed on acid-free paper. ⊗

Copyright © 1999 by Upside Magazine. All rights reserved.

Published by John Wiley & Sons, Inc.

Published simultaneously in Canada.

No part of this publication may be reproduced, stored in a retrieval system or transmitted in any form or by any means, electronic, mechanical, photocopying, recording, scanning or otherwise, except as permitted under Sections 107 or 108 of the 1976 United States Copyright Act, without either the prior written permission of the Publisher, or authorization through payment of the appropriate per-copy fee to the Copyright Clearance Center, 222 Rosewood Drive, Danvers, MA 01923, (978) 750-8400, fax (978) 750-4744. Requests to the Publisher for permission should be addressed to the Permissions Department, John Wiley & Sons, Inc., 605 Third Avenue, New York, NY 10158-0012, (212) 850-6011, fax (212) 850-6008, E-Mail: PERMREQ@WILEY.COM.

This publication is designed to provide accurate and authoritative information in regard to the subject matter covered. It is sold with the understanding that the publisher is not engaged in rendering legal, accounting, or other professional services. If legal advice or other expert assistance is required, the services of a competent professional person should be sought.

Library of Congress Cataloging-in-Publication Data:

Southwick, Karen.
    Silicon gold rush : the next generation of high-tech stars rewrites the rules of business / Karen Southwick.
        p.   cm.
    Includes index.
    ISBN 0-471-24646-8 (cloth : alk. paper)
    1. Computer industry—Management.   2. Computer software industry—Management.   3. High technology industries—Management.   4. New business enterprises—Management.   I. Title.
    HD9696.2.A2S67   1998
    338.4'7004—dc21   98-24359
                                                                                     CIP

Printed in the United States of America.

10 9 8 7 6 5 4 3 2 1

Contents

Foreword

By Geoffrey Moore

Surging beneath the chorus of voices that Karen Southwick has assembled on the following pages is the relentless undercurrent of breathlessness and urgency that lies at the very heart of the place and state of mind known as Silicon Valley. Pressing forward daily, hourly, this frenetic sense of speed and change permeates the entire technology industry, and it is the single most pervasive trait among all the companies profiled in this book. Once it gets into the bloodstream, it doesn't leave. The venture capitalists have it. The entrepreneurs have it. The engineers have it. The service providers have it.

But here's the rub: For the most part, the technology industry's customers do not have it. Oh, a few do—the early adopters, the ones who get courted over and over again—but the average person, be it a services client, a business customer, or a home-based consumer—simply is not in this kind of hurry. So there is a fundamental mismatch between the pacing of the technology industry and that of the people who must ultimately fund its concoctions.

This raises an overriding question about the Silicon Valley business model: If there is such a great mismatch, why and how has the model been so successful? More to the point, is it a temporary aberration or is it an abiding shift in management approach? This book provides the reader with insights about the model that may help answer those important questions. How the country as a whole responds to this, and how the technology industry itself steps up to its future, will have economic consequences for decades to come.

Let's do away with some simplistic answers. Like, "the customer is always right." Wrong. The customer is a good guide when companies are making continuous improvements to existing technologies. But customers are *not* a good guide when the product is a discontinuous innovation, something which will require major systems reengineering to bring about, which will "change the world as we know it." When asked about such innovations, customers typically say "Great!" during focus groups—and then stay away in droves when it comes time to purchase. In both venues their feedback is simply not useful. As Silicon Valley spends the bulk of its time on just these kinds of products, it has abandoned the steady-as-you-go research and test-market approach to new-market development, and instead runs off spouting its "Ready, Fire, Aim!" philosophy to anyone who will listen. Using memorable anecdotes and profiles, *Silicon Gold Rush* ably demonstrates how this model functions.

But how right can "Ready, Fire, Aim!" really be? Well, surprisingly, pretty darn right—as long as we are dealing in the domain of truly discontinuous innovations. The challenge in this domain is that at the outset there are no known targets or guideposts. The only navigational aid is your own trajectory, and the sooner you start that trajectory—regardless of how inappropriately directed it is—the better off you are. Only after it is started can customers react in a meaningful way to what you have, after which you can begin to see how your trajectory must be altered to truly intersect with their wants and needs. It is a course in white-water rafting, not transoceanic navigation, that is being taught in Silicon Valley, Boston, Seattle, and other high-tech strongholds.

And that's just fine, until you reach the ocean—the broader domain of continuous improvement to established systems, the world of traditional business. It is here that Silicon Valley will be challenged during the coming decade. No other place on the planet has had more success in market formation and in the generation of market capitalization. But both these disciplines are forward-looking. Both imply that one can assign stock-market value today to competitive advantages that must be executed against tomorrow. Silicon Valley companies have been unmatched in their ability to generate extraordinary competitive advantages that, if market valuations are to be believed, will give them above average returns for six, eight, ten years to come. I for one believe those advantages are indeed sustainable over those periods—but only if the cultures that bred them can step up to the challenge of becoming enduring institutions.

Here I pause. For I myself do not like the breathlessness of Silicon Valley. I do not like its hyperconnected communications style. I do not like its insistence on being young and hip and hot and hyped. I have this vision of Thoreau and Emerson and Whitman and Dickinson, all calling out to us, all trying to wave us away from some collision course with—what? I do not know. But I am nervous about it.

Here is where I think the significance of *Silicon Gold Rush* comes in. We are indeed in the midst of a gold rush, with all the implications that phrase calls to mind. Such good fortune does limit one's options—you cannot go slowly on the way to Sutter's Mill and expect to find much when you get there. The pace is forced by the situation, as much now as it was 150 years ago. And that pace, in turn, has brought into existence new patterns of wealth formation, new ways to partner and compete, new modes of recruiting, managing, and retaining employees, new ways of conceiving the employment relationship. In the context of hypergrowth markets, I believe these new modes are right on the mark, so the world around the technology industry should take note and take notes.

And after? Well, there's still a lot of here-and-now to get through first, but one thing is sure: The strategy of standing back, of holding these new methods in disdain, of disassociating oneself and one's enterprise from them, causes failure. In business as in football, the West Coast offense is here to stay, and the East Coast establishment and other economies around the world must absorb it and respond to it, not reject it. Reading and reacting to the ideas in this book is a great way to start. But in so doing, each of these other economies needs to find its own expression of the insights accumulated here, one that integrates traditional strength with new learning. We do not need a Silicon Prairie or Silicon Forest or Silicon Alley—drop the silicon. We need some new element from the periodic table. As Silicon Valley pundits frequently like to note (attributing the notion to Picasso), "Great artists do not copy—they steal!"

Finally, for those of us who live and work in Silicon Valley, this book is a currency check. The ideas in it are what's happening today. If they are unfamiliar to you, get with them. If you think you've "got" them, you're getting jaded and you'd better look again. There are still a lot of miracles to come from Silicon Valley.

Geoffrey Moore is chairman of The Chasm Group, a consulting firm in San Mateo, California, and a venture partner in Mohr Davidow Ventures. He is author of *Crossing the Chasm, Inside the Tornado,* and *The Gorilla Game: An Investor's Guide to Picking Winners in High Tech.*

Introduction

The New Gold Rush

In January 1848, gold nuggets were first discovered in the American River near the town of Coloma, California. The effects of that discovery were felt for decades after. It was not just a matter of the wealth generated by the mining of the precious metal itself (more than $2 billion worth before it was depleted). The gold industry caused a whole infrastructure of other industries to spring up around it—employing suppliers and partners and advisers and distributors and assayers and many others. It even hastened statehood for California. Just as important, the gold rush helped to seed the idea that it is possible—through a combination of good luck, hard work, and technology—to get rich quickly. Tens of thousands of would-be millionaires poured into California from all over the world. But very few of these miners actually struck it rich: They found that the work was tougher than they had expected and that the chances of any individual hitting it big were very small.

In 1998, 150 years later, we are experiencing a similar frenzy of commercial activity that I call the "Silicon Gold Rush"—meaning the industries and companies and markets that have sprung up around the essential ingredient of the digital revolution, silicon. It, too, originated in Cali-

fornia, and centers now in the companies of Silicon Valley, south of San Francisco, although there are significant
outposts in areas like Seattle, Boston, New York, and
Austin, Texas. Just as the California Gold Rush opened a
whole new market and created a whole new mindset, so
the Silicon Gold Rush has changed the face of American
(and global) industry, and spawned the creation of a set of
industries and businesses that support and surround it.
Equally as important, the companies involved in the Silicon Gold Rush structure themselves and conduct their
business in substantially—even radically—different ways
than companies that we think of as "traditional," by which
I mean the divisionalized hierarchies that have been the
norm in this country for many decades.

The success of these silicon-based companies—from
the tiniest start-up to the grandfather of them all, Hewlett-
Packard—has deeply influenced traditional organizations
and forced them to think about, and often adopt, the new
ways of operating. Everywhere you look today, older companies and those in traditional industries are adopting the
organizational structures, business strategies, and operational methods of the Silicon Valley gang. In other words,
the technology companies are changing more than the
markets in which they operate—they are transforming the
way America does business.

In this book, I explore these new structures, strategies,
and methods through the stories of 23 technology companies, most of them based in Silicon Valley itself. For a
number of reasons I have chosen a start-up venture, Cross-
Worlds Software, to take a starring role in the book. The
story of this fledgling corporation contains many of the
elements that make the technology industry so exciting
and instructive to watch. They include the scramble for financing. The glitzy launch events. The feverish jamming
to move the initial product from design to manufacture
and into the hands of paying customers. The "spin cycle"—
the combination of self-promotion and media hype that
can create a perception of momentum—even before there

is actual movement. The colorful cast of characters. The nontraditional work environment. The high stakes and big money. The meteoric growth. The constant risk of failure, radical change, takeover, buyout, and burnout.

I have been following the silicon scene and the companies that compose it for more than a decade, first as a business writer for the *San Francisco Chronicle* and, over the past six years, with *Upside* magazine. It has been fascinating and thought-provoking to get to know these companies intimately, through repeated visits to their sites, interviews with key players both inside and outside the companies, and through my research into their pasts, their performance, and their prospects.

My goal for this book has been to synthesize what I have observed over the past decade and what I have learned in more than 100 in-depth interviews with executives of the 23 companies and with other knowledgeable observers of high technology. The result is 10 chapters and a conclusion, each of which focuses on a key issue that pertains to all of these companies, to a greater or lesser degree, and that also has relevance to businesses and organizations outside the world of technology. The book is organized as follows:

➤ Chapter 1 provides an overview of the silicon environment, its size, scope, potential, and values through the experience of launching a start-up company.

➤ In Chapter 2, I examine the changing role of the key leader, usually the CEO. In technology companies, the CEO tends to play a far different role than the chief executive of a big, traditional hierarchy.

➤ In Chapter 3, I talk about the special concerns of small companies that want to grow fast but without losing their entrepreneurial spark in the process.

➤ Chapter 4 explores the paradox of large technology companies that seek to leverage the power of their size while also maintaining the attitude of small-ness and retaining the flexibility and speed that characterized them in their early days.

➤ Chapter 5 describes how technology companies must stake out markets early, and be prepared to re-define them on the turn of a dime.

➤ In Chapter 6, I talk about this strange and wonderful "spin cycle" that can create momentum for an un-known company virtually overnight. Today, it goes beyond the standard mix of press coverage, trade shows, special events, and advertising—it requires new ways to involve partners and customers and key influencers in creating an image and building a reputation.

➤ Chapter 7 shows how the customer has become deeply integrated into the development and mar-keting processes of technology companies. No longer is there a gap between supplier and cus-tomer. Indeed, today's toughest skeptic can be to-morrow's best customer.

➤ In Chapter 8, I look at the way technology compa-nies organize themselves internally and go about getting work done. Company culture involves far more than the color scheme of headquarters or the dogs romping in the cubicles. It's about how mem-bers of the company think of themselves and how they form, define, and manage relationships among themselves.

➤ Chapter 9 focuses on one of the most intriguing as-pects of the technology industry: the mergers and alliances that are a constant feature. Why do these companies find it necessary to buy, merge, sell, and consume each other? What makes for a successful merger? What can lead to failure?

➤ In Chapter 10, I dispel the notion that success is guaranteed in the technology industry, by examining companies that made a wrong turn and are now trying to get back on track. More than half of technology start-ups ultimately fail. What are the most common catastrophes that befall technology companies? What can they do to improve their chances of survival?

➤ The conclusion revisits the start-up company that we introduced in Chapter 1.

I've written this book for executives, managers, and observers of technology and nontechnology industries alike because, increasingly, *all* global business is caught up in the rush generated by the high-technology ventures. It is a rush of activity that directly involves computers and all the associated software and services that surround it. It is a rush to move communications and customer interaction and sales to the Internet, the newest field of dreams. It is also a rush generated by the amazing and pervasive changes and innovations that the technology companies have brought to the world. And, finally, it is a rush simply because it is so fast-paced and so intellectually intoxicating that no businessperson can escape its power.

I hope that you sense—and benefit from—the excitement coursing through these pages.

Chapter

1

A Star Is Born

The best way to understand the power and potential of Silicon Valley technology companies today is to examine how they are conceived and born. It used to be that new companies were founded by scrappy entrepreneurs—often with little or no business experience—in a garage or warehouse, with little or no capital. Some new companies still emerge that way, but it is no longer the most common or desirable way to get started.

Consider the "launch" party of CrossWorlds Software, a technology start-up based in Burlingame, California, a community on the northern edge of Silicon Valley. The lavish party takes place in June 1997, and its cost probably exceeds the entire seed capital of many an earlier start-up. It is held not in a garage or a warehouse, but on the 15th floor of the Merchants Exchange Building in San Francisco's financial district. The event has been planned and is being coordinated by a production firm hired by Cross-Worlds. A four-piece jazz band plays. Scores of hostesses scurry about, greeting distinguished guests, pinning on name tags, and escorting people to the bar.

The party has succeeded in attracting an audience of industry heavyweights and influencers—the men and women who have helped turn many a silicon dream into reality. The well-known executives from the high-profile technology companies arrive later than most of the other guests. The first of the executives to enter the room is Andy Ludwick, who has managed two major technology companies, Bay Networks and SynOptics. Others include Dave Stamm, John Luongo, and Joe Liemandt, all software company presidents; and financial mogul Frank Quattrone of DMG Technology Group, whose pronouncements can sink a company or raise it to new heights. The energy in the room is palpable. Casual conversations, both business and social, pulsate with the intensity of an industry whose wealth, power, and the potential for expansion and explosive growth are seemingly unlimited. The guests have come to listen and learn, to schmooze, and to size up CrossWorlds as a potential partner or investment.

CrossWorlds' tagline for the event is simple and prodigious: "We're entering the promised land." The promised land it refers to, of course, is the territory staked out by the likes of Microsoft, Netscape, and Cisco Systems—companies that have developed powerful technologies, opened up new markets, generated billions of dollars in market value and revenues, created thousands of jobs, turned hundreds of employees and investors into millionaires, and even changed the way business is conducted. Every day, in the technology capitals of Silicon Valley, Seattle, Boston, and Austin, entrepreneurs and investors get together to hatch the big idea that they hope will eventually become the next Microsoft or Intel.

At 5:00 P.M., the hostesses finish seating the hundreds of guests in a presentation room adjoining the reception area. The lights dim on the elaborate stage. The chatter dies and a video appears on the center screen. It features prominent technology leaders and opinion shapers, including Peter Kastner from Aberdeen Group, as well as executives like Dave Duffield and Heinz Roggen-Kemper from respected behemoths PeopleSoft and SAP AG, respectively. Their role is to describe and praise CrossWorlds' technology.

Part of the video features an interview with Cross-Worlds' founder and chief executive, Katrina Garnett, conducted by local TV host Brian Banmiller. Garnett is polished, attractive, and articulate, and exudes an air of confidence, experience, and knowledge. Garnett spent 10 years with Oracle and Sybase, two important players in the hotly competitive database industry. When she left Sybase to found CrossWorlds, she was a general manager/vice president. Garnett and her husband, Terry, have committed $5.5 million of their own money to the development and founding of CrossWorlds. They have also raised funds from several prestigious investors, including Venrock Associates—the Rockefeller family's venture fund—and the accounting powerhouse Ernst & Young, along with companies such as Compaq, SAP, and Intel. In all, CrossWorlds has amassed more than $46.6 million in capital, which puts it in the top tier of private financing. The average amount raised by a software start-up in 1997 was only $4.9 million, according to VentureOne Corporation of San Francisco.

Garnett explains to Banmiller that she wants to build a major software company to serve what she believes is a new and important market niche, which she calls "processware." As Garnett describes it, Fortune 1000 corporations have been spending billions installing "front-end" systems that run solutions for customer support, payment, and sales. They also have invested heavily in "back-end" systems that handle human resources, manufacturing, and accounting applications. But the front end and back end don't always connect or communicate smoothly with each other, she says, and this can prove troublesome—even disastrous—for companies that need to operate as seamlessly as possible. CrossWorlds' products make communication between these systems not only possible, but relatively effortless.

Garnett outlines the potential market value of Cross-Worlds' products by describing the success of the first processware release with test clients such as Hewlett-Packard and Bay Networks. These industry titans were so pleased with the performance of early "beta" versions of CrossWorlds' product that they helped the company further develop and prepare it for general release. Garnett closes the interview with the kind of hyperbole that flows in Silicon Valley like wine flows in the Napa Valley. "We're going to go where no one has gone before," she declares.

After Garnett's appearance, DMG Technology Group analyst George Gilbert talks numbers. According to his estimate, the $13 billion market for front-end and back-end application software will grow to the $40 to $50 billion range in the next five years. Processware, Gilbert predicts, could capture as much as 10 percent of that market. That's $4 billion!

The presentation ends to thunderous applause. The guests drift back to the bar to analyze, imagine, connive, and consider the promise of CrossWorlds.

■ DRIVING AT BREAKNECK SPEED

CrossWorlds' initial product could, as predicted, achieve enormous sales. But as successful as the launch appeared to be, it provides no guarantee that the company will live a long and happy life. The founders might have guessed wrong about the importance of the envisioned niche, or about its size. Or the company may suffer problems with manufacturing or product performance. Or its technology could be copied by a rival or a partner, who will outmarket and outsell CrossWorlds and demolish it. But the birth and early childhood of the company reflect how the high-tech industry operates. Technological innovation drives explosive growth that fuels greater competition, thereby creating a need for more advanced technology. And so it goes. This pattern can be attributed to any global business operating in a competitive industry.

The continual emergence of new products as well as new companies accelerates the frantically spinning treadmill that the technology industry is on. Like the Red

Queen in *Alice in Wonderland,* even mature, well-established companies such as Microsoft have to run ever faster just to maintain their position. The unbridled growth and fierce competitive nature of the high-tech industry demands that management respond immediately to every new turn and development with a variety of strategies, all the while assuring employees and investors that the company has a long-term goal. "High-tech companies operate like they're on a CNN floor, with breaking news every ten minutes," says Ann Winblad, a partner with Hummer Winblad Venture Partners of San Francisco, a leading investor in software start-ups. A former entrepreneur herself, Winblad is one of the most highly regarded venture capitalists in the high-tech industry and is widely known for her ability to pick winners, including Arbor Software and Wind River Systems.

In business, winners are largely recognized by strong leadership, flexible organizational structure, and egalitarian management style. Successful high-tech companies, like those profiled in this book, cultivate their own innovative spirit to create award-winning products, open new markets, advance innovation, and effectively manage the organization—and they do this in the midst of a frenetic, hypercompetitive environment. The technology industry is largely the result of innovations and approaches introduced only recently. Gary Hamel is chairman of Strategos, a consulting company in Woodside, California, and coauthor of *Competing for the Future,* which describes ways that companies and industries can reshape themselves to compete more effectively. "The future is not created by prophets, it's created by heretics, people who have a different industrial model," proclaims Hamel. "In the sense that a lot of the future is driven by what becomes possible technically, people who are able to reconfigure an industry in some new way will be successful." It is the heretics who are willing to tear down the status quo, to eliminate the hierarchical management and command-and-control mentality in favor of a new, still-emerging model.

TEN COMMANDMENTS FOR NEXT-GENERATION BUSINESSES

1. *Shape the company's culture and work ethic.* A shared vision and corporate culture must flow from the top. The CEO must inspire people to join in a greater cause, managing and nurturing the company's knowledge capital.
2. *Maintain a fresh perspective.* Look at your company's place in the world as something ephemeral and transitory rather than assured and permanent. That point of view enables you to embrace change itself as constant and to evolve the qualities required to become an agent of change rather than its victim.
3. *Cultivate knowledge.* Distribute the company's leadership throughout the organization so that each employee is entrusted with higher levels of responsibility and information management—thus satisfying not only monetary needs, but higher-level needs such as self-fulfillment as well.
4. *Develop mind share.* Mind share is a calculated campaign to influence the influencers. To capture mind share—and the most market visibility—complement the company's product innovation with brand marketing initiatives. Proclaim yourself the market leader by leading a paradigm shift, establishing a standard, or positioning yourself as an industry authority.
5. *Eschew formal structures and be a team!* Form teams to decide how to allocate resources, prioritize tasks, and determine a schedule to launch the product. Senior management acts much like a venture capital investor, assessing the merits of relative projects, assigning values, selecting the teams (or at least the team leader), and giving them budgets and

(continued)

TEN COMMANDMENTS FOR NEXT-GENERATION BUSINESSES (Continued)

deadlines. This team concept allows for the high level of flexibility that's essential in the fast-paced high-tech industry.

6. *The customer, not the technology, is #1.* Leading companies tailor their products to meet real customer needs. As soon as a blueprint is ready, customers are invited to give feedback and design advice.

7. *Find the right partners, mergers, and acquisitions.* Technology companies have become more outwardly focused on devising relationships with customers and with prospective alliance and merger partners. In an acquisition, core internal values must be unified among the business partners. Make your company an integral part of a web of relationships, enhancing internal and external growth.

8. *Embrace the unknown.* Even as you're mining your own claim, be ready for the next gold rush, which could occur in an entirely unexpected place. Maybe you can't forecast the location of a new strike, but you can create a company that can move anywhere.

9. *Be paranoid.* The competitive environment in the high-tech industry won't let anyone relax. Know that as soon as you innovate a successful product, you will face a horde of aspiring competitors and must be prepared to act (hence Commandment #10).

10. *Be a speed demon and don't be squeamish.* Technology itself, and the companies that create it, are combining to usher in a new era where management styles and structures are being remade on the fly. Ultimately, what keeps a company going is the vision to cope with speed of market change, technological advances, and emerging business opportunities.

"The future is not created by prophets, it's created by heretics, people who have a different industrial model."
—Gary Hamel, coauthor of *Competing for the Future*

■ LEVELING THE PLAYING FIELD

Technology has the unique ability to eliminate barriers to better business, whether they be related to costs, logistics, productivity, or the market. High-technology companies are particularly adept at tearing down the boundaries found in conventional businesses. "Traditionally, you built your company around some sustainable advantage—proximity to the market or a regulated monopoly or patents," says Joe K. Carter, office managing partner in technology for Andersen Consulting LLP in Palo Alto, California. "Technology is in the process of eliminating all of those." Powerful networking technology allows experts from all corners of the globe to collaborate on a specific project, obliterating proximity barriers. With technological innovation moving ahead at warp speed and savvy entrepreneurs creating new markets, the barriers to financial support have diminished. In fact, the industry is awash in money as never before. In 1996, venture capital firms invested $5.4 billion in 962 information technology start-ups, double what they had invested just two years earlier, according to VentureOne. And 1997 saw $7.1 billion flowing to 1,095 deals. Money from these sources is joined by largesse from the previous generation of technology entrepreneurs, people like Bill Gates and Steve Jobs who, as "angel" investors, push portions of their huge hoards of personal wealth back into the industry they know best.

High-tech companies are among the first to take advantage of technology solutions, enabling them to focus more intently on their products and how these products serve customers. With the playing field somewhat leveled given the availability of technology, what can a company do to reach the top of the pack? "You have to innovate faster than the other guys and you have to execute even more quickly," says Carter. The primary sustainable advantage, then, is speed of execution, which technology companies have elevated to cult status in their efforts to run farther and faster than anyone else. Boasts Gideon Gartner, chairman and chief executive of Giga Information Group in Norwell, Massachusetts: "In our industry segment—information services—it's possible to invent a new service, announce it, and start delivering it within 24 hours. We would like to be able to change something as quickly as you can put it on the Web."

"Markets move so quickly that building any kind of bureaucracy is suicide. Anything that slows down product development has to be cast aside."
—Geoffrey James, author of *Business Wisdom of the Electronic Elite*

■ READY, FIRE, AIM!

Speed and competitiveness are closely intertwined. Regis McKenna, legendary technology marketing strategist and founder of The McKenna Group in Palo Alto, refers to this interconnection as "the continual cauldron of competitive pressure." This means that the companies that are fastest to market with viable products have the best chance of survival. One management model equates this cauldron-like environment to a living ecosystem where the competitive pressure acts as a Darwinian imperative, forcing companies to make evolutionary leaps at a much faster pace than would otherwise occur. For a technology company, this means that the business must not only keep pace with change, but find a way to anticipate it. "You have to understand trends, how enabling technologies are advancing, and what other complementary technologies might create customer value," says

Jim Moore, chief executive of C
bridge, Massachusetts, and aut.
tion, which expands on the busi

and the fina
and gen
ageri
u

"Each time there's an order-of-
ways you can use technology ch
customer base changes, too."
——Jim Moore, founder c
of   ...,petition

To stand still in this new world is death. Digital Equipment is a perfect example of this axiom. A highly regarded
innovator of minicomputers (think "mainframe light")
during the 1970s and 1980s, the company faltered when its
management could not cope with the evolutionary leap to
the personal computer. Today, Digital has become part of
PC-maker Compaq Computer Corporation. Digital's experience proves that moving forward is vital, even if, like the
one-celled creature that first lifted itself out of the primor-
dial soup, you don't quite know where you're moving. "Previously, you wanted to develop a detailed business plan or
blueprint," notes John Hagel III, a principal with consultant McKinsey & Company in Palo Alto and coauthor of
Net Gain. "Now," he adds, "you draw on outside disciplines,
like complex adaptive systems or genetic algorithms. Instead of thinking about strategy as a detailed blueprint,
you define a set of basic and limited rules that will drive
your actions. Then you rapidly act upon those rules and
discard the ones that don't have a lot of success." Instead of
ready, aim, fire!, it's ready, fire, aim!

As a result, the technology industry, like any frontier,
has attracted a new type of executive and a new type of
employee—indeed, the two are almost indistinguishable.
The key attributes of both include a tolerance for chaos,
disdain for hierarchy and politicking, willingness to fail,
elevation of talent and brilliance, passion for technology,
and naivete about limits. Thanks to a booming job market

ncial freedom created by equity participation
rous salaries and bonuses, the traditional man-
l structure in high-tech companies has been turned
side down.

■ EMPLOYEES RULE THE ROOST

Consultant, writer, and high-tech philosopher Michael Rothschild is also an advocate of the business-as-biology model.
He has pursued this approach through his work at the Bio-
nomics Institute in San Francisco and is implementing the
framework as president and chief executive of Maxager
Technology in nearby San Rafael. Rothschild believes that
economic power has always rested in the hands of those
who control leverageable assets. It used to be rent, then it
was machinery. Today it's information and knowledge—
which are no longer the exclusive provinces of management. "People who have the brainpower and skills get to
call their own shots," says Rothschild. "They can live where
they want and with the lifestyle they want. It's damn close
to full personal freedom. If I piss off my employees, within
an hour they've got six job offers. If I tell them to stop playing computer games, they would say, 'f--- you,' and leave."

Realizing this, savvy managers engage these take-me-
or-leave-me employees personally by binding them to the
company's success through stock options and other incentives, which act as a means of sharing both the risk and reward. Technology companies founded in the 1970s and
1980s, like Intel, Microsoft, Oracle, and Cisco, have made
millionaires of thousands of their employees—and not
just the executives, but also receptionists, assistants, marketing managers, and human resource directors. "The secret of Microsoft is that everybody becomes a millionaire
after a certain period of time," says Robert Reid, a principal at 21st Century Internet Venture Partners in San Francisco. Equity—participation in the company through

stock options—is now ground zero for hiring at technology companies. It's proven to be a curse for companies as well as a blessing. "As the bidding for talent goes up, everyone has to offer more," says Reid. "The alternative is to focus on the work environment to a greater extent."

Equity—participation in the company through stock options—is now ground zero for hiring at technology companies.

The concept of employee ownership has become the foundation of technology companies. It is the way in which companies compete for the knowledge worker, who is seeking not just the weekly paycheck, food-on-the-table job security of the past but the skill-expanding job security of the future. Famed psychologist Abraham Maslow would find proof of his theories within high-tech companies. Maslow's hierarchy of needs sets up humanity's requirements as a pyramid, starting with physiological needs at the base and proceeding to higher needs, such as esteem and self-actualization. In the high-technology arena, as well as other knowledge-based industries, the basic needs have been satisfied; only the higher ones remain to be fulfilled. These include involvement in satisfying work, influence over the end-product, and a sense that what you do has some impact on your company, your customers, and your industry.

Walk into almost any high-tech company and you typically will find employees in casual dress; foosball tables sharing space with the refrigerator (well-stocked with Cokes) in the kitchen; prominently placed containers of free candy (all that sugar gives you a short-term rush); knots of people engaged in seemingly random, animated discussions; walls bearing photos of pets, family members, and coworkers; cubicle workspaces marked with interchangeable nameplates; and cutely titled conference rooms, sometimes named after theme parks or biblical plagues, available on a first-come, first-serve basis. Employees and executives are indistinguishable: The 25-year-old pounding away at a computer is as likely to be the chief executive as the 40-year-old hunched over a spreadsheet. The guy who picks up the ringing phone that no one else answered could be the chief financial officer, the one carrying in pizza the vice president of human resources. What you will not see are executive suites, preferred parking spaces, personal secretaries, and fancy office furniture.

The fluidity of knowledge transfer has contributed to blurring the boundaries between executive and employee in other ways as well. In the past, the person who had access to the most information sat at the top of the heap. But now, in the age of the Internet, information has become so abundant and accessible that everyone swims in it. The hallmark of the successful high-tech executive is not withholding information, but making sense of it, and then ensuring that everyone in the company has the information that he or she needs to work at maximum productivity.

Such a business exemplifies the truly "flattened" organization, where the concept of employee ownership is taken seriously and given equal weight within the organization. But when companies attempt to apply the principles of employee ownership without fully understanding the sensibilities underlying the approach, that attempt falls short. In such a case, the end result may be a company where functional jobs have become so blurred that it is difficult for employees to understand their role and thereby take responsibility for it.

"The aligned organization achieves its purposes without hierarchy and with little micro-management. It has an 'invisible hand of culture and systems that keeps everyone doing the right things right.'"

—George Labovitz and Victor Rosansky in
The Power of Alignment

■ LASER-LIKE INTENSITY

One of the many ironies that permeate the technology industry is that as your vision becomes ever more expansive, your company focus must become narrower and narrower, something like a laser beam. One formula for failure is to spread yourself too thin. Seemingly limitless market opportunities abound, particularly when you're led by a visionary whose very dreams are made up of ideas that multiply like sheep and may scatter as quickly. Pinpointing the unexploited opportunity that could develop into a large market is the first challenge for any executive, manager, or entrepreneur. Cisco, for example, parlayed a simple idea—so-called routers that act like traffic cops in directing electronic data to a desired point—into a multibillion-dollar business in less than a decade. CrossWorlds is trying to emulate that with its notion of processware.

"The most important thing, particularly for a startup, is to become highly focused," says Jim Breyer, managing partner at Accel Partners, a San Francisco–based venture capital firm. "There's a danger to thinking too big and not getting the first product right. Get the first product right and it serves as a platform for the rest of your growth."

Focus extends to processes as well. Many technology companies outsource public relations, human resources, sales and marketing, even financial management in order to concentrate on developing a product. This approach allows the company to stick to its "core competencies," a strategy popularized by authors Hamel and Prahalad in their book *Competing for the Future*. This strategy extends to larger, more established companies, too. In fact, the outsourcing of manufacturing, recruiting, marketing, and communications functions has become so pervasive in the technology industry that these services have become huge growth segments themselves.

> "A core competence is a bundle of skills and technologies that enables a company to provide a particular benefit to customers."
> —Gary Hamel and C.K. Prahalad in *Competing for the Future*

A company today is augmented by the extended web it has spun around itself, consisting of suppliers, resellers, technology partners, customers, and even competitors. Customers contribute to financing product development, work with engineers on-site, suggest design changes, and help promote the finished item. One large company, Veri-Fone, headquartered in Redwood City, California, describes itself as a "virtual" company in which location is immaterial and executives, employees, and divisions are scattered across the country and the world. Anything that would tie the company to a specific site, like manufacturing, is handled by external partners. VeriFone has realized that every competitor in one sphere of technology is a collaborator in another; the universe of technology applications is expanding so fast and so unpredictably that no one company can possibly keep up by itself. It's clear that a company must be singularly focused on its own mission, even while its outer bounds are growing increasingly fuzzy.

■ TELLING A HIGH-TECH SUCCESS STORY

In the technology industry as in life, perception can shape reality. Your company launches a product, identifies a new market for it, invites the gurus such as the Meta Group, Forrester Group, Yankee Group, or other leading industry analysts to pronounce their blessing, and quicker than you can say "amen," you're the market leader. It doesn't matter if no one else is in the market yet, or if the market has yet to clearly materialize—you're the leader and you've got mind share. Being the market leader, no matter how elusive or undefined the market, gives you clout when you talk to potential buyers and seek out partners to repackage your product and distributors to sell it.

Geoffrey Moore, a Palo Alto–based consultant and the author of the best-selling books *Crossing the Chasm* and *Inside the Tornado,* credits Regis McKenna with masterminding one of the earliest and best campaigns for capturing mind share. Back in the 1980s, "the Regis Touch" transformed what was then a relatively small and unknown company, Apple Computer, into a big-time publicity machine. McKenna wove the combination of trade show appearances, startling TV ads, pronouncements by industry gurus, and press releases presaging even the smallest advance or alliance into the buzz that surrounds high tech today. This strategy continues to work today, as *Time* anoints Microsoft's Bill Gates as the second-most-powerful man in the world (after the president of the United States) and picks Intel's Andy Grove as its 1997 Man of the Year, and as the values of high-tech companies and products skyrocket.

Unfortunately, high tech has been too successful at its own game. There's so much noise surrounding so many products that even McKenna decries it now. "Apple has the greatest mind share in the industry," he notes, "and where has it gotten them?" Too many technology companies are trying to build mind share before they have infrastructure to support it. "Young companies think mind share comes first and that's a mistake," he says. "You build the infrastructure first. If you do the mind-share thing and you don't have the infrastructure, you go out of business."

Another important tactic for becoming a known market leader is to partner with companies that already have mind share. "You move for ubiquity before you worry about revenues," says venture capitalist Reid. To that end, "partnerships are very important. Identify the king-maker in your area and become their first and greatest friend." The catch-22 of having partners to codevelop or comarket your technology is that they could become competitors or unwelcome acquirers. Everyone in the industry likes to hook up with Microsoft. You link yourself to the big kahuna and you get a few minutes in the spotlight. Later, though, the big kahuna may swallow you up.

■ THE FATHER TO US ALL

The goal of this book is to unveil the management approaches and business strategies of successful companies operating in what is arguably the most competitive business environment to date. To do this, it makes sense to look at those who have laid the foundation for today's high-tech titans.

Perhaps the earliest and greatest precursor of today's emerging technology management style is Hewlett-Packard. HP has been well chronicled in numerous books, including *The HP Way: How Bill Hewlett and I Built Our Company* by the late cofounder David Packard. While this book will not attempt to tread across old ground, it would be unfair not to acknowledge the looming influence of Hewlett and Packard's notions of "management by walking around"—decentralization, informality, creativity, and trust for employees, principles now carried on by successor generations of management.

HP has withstood the test of time by remaking itself from an engineering-driven company into a marketing-driven one, and by moving into new markets like printers and personal computers (where it recently served notice it wants to be number one by 2001), all the while retaining a set of core values that animate everything it does. "The high-tech industry genuflects at the feet of HP," says Howard Anderson, founder and president of The Yankee Group and founder of Battery Ventures, both in Boston. "With industrial America, General Electric Company was the template. In high tech we're all children or grandchildren of the HP management school. No one in the long haul has been able to finesse high tech as well as HP. It's the West Coast offense," he says, referring to the finesse passing game perfected by the San Francisco 49ers under former coach Bill Walsh.

Another example of lasting influence comes from the "Fairchild Eight"—Robert Noyce and seven other scientists who left Bell Labs in 1957 to found Fairchild Semiconductor and who in doing so planted the seeds of what would become Silicon Valley. The man who headed the Bell Labs outpost in California, physicist William Shockley, intended to build on his knowledge of transistor electronics. But Shockley, for all his technological brilliance, was a traditional manager who distrusted his employees. "Shockley wanted to run everything as a hierarchy," recalls Regis McKenna. "It was an us-versus-them environment. Noyce and the others left that strict environment to start Fairchild. They selected Noyce as their leader and got venture capital. That became the model." In 1968, Noyce teamed up with Gordon Moore to found Intel Corporation, developer of the microprocessor, which kicked off the digital revolution.

Intel and Microsoft, who together form the feared and respected "Wintel" alliance that overwhelmingly dominates the personal computer industry, honed a more paranoid approach to management than HP. Wintel emphasized extreme competition internally and externally, even pitting employees' ideas against each other in acerbic verbal jousts. Going to the other extreme, there is much-maligned Apple, which has frittered away its advantages but, in the mid-1980s, represented the epitome of high-tech creativity and fanatic devotion to a cause greater than oneself. "The only true revolutionaries in Silicon Valley were Steve Jobs and Noyce," says Don Valentine, who was with Noyce at Fairchild and later founded Sequoia Capital in Menlo Park, California, one of the first venture capital firms and an early investor in Apple. "Everything else is evolutionary." In more than a quarter-century of investing in Silicon Valley, Valentine has seen most of the industry's evolution.

Wintel, HP, and Apple represent the various extremes that constitute the boundaries of today's high-tech management style. Each has a dark side. From Wintel come the notions of hypercompetitiveness and reliance upon the best and the brightest to fuel an insatiable appetite for dominance. But in running roughshod over competitors and arm-twisting customers to use their products, Microsoft and Intel have both drawn scrutiny from U.S. antitrust enforcers. From HP comes the more gentlemanly school of loyalty, empowerment, and decentralized decision-making. However, HP's consensus-driven model is not known for swiftness of execution, and it usually enters new markets after they're already established by someone smaller and more nimble. From Apple comes the passion and the vision—*this is the right thing to do regardless of what all the idiots think*—that led to breakthroughs like the Macintosh personal computer. Such arrogance, taken too far by a succession of CEOs, resulted in precisely the situation Apple faces now: declining market share and a desperate fight for survival. Ideally, a technology company today should be able to mix-and-match these management styles, perhaps exercising Apple-like fanaticism to win converts to a new product, Microsoft muscle to build market dominance, and HP ethics to polish its image.

■ ADVENT OF THE NET

To bring the story fully up to date, we must stir into this mix of disparate influences the proliferation of the Internet as tool and culture, and the entrance of the first generation who grew up with computers: Generation-Xers. Not coincidentally, Gen-Xers are often the ones who start Internet companies, which make tools or content designed to exploit the new medium. The Internet, and e-mail, facilitate the instant communication with anyone anytime

EXPERT OPINION

Geoffrey James, Executive Director of the Institute for Business Wisdom, Hollis, New Hampshire, and author of *Business Wisdom of the Electronic Elite*

On Structure:

"Markets move so quickly that building any kind of bureaucracy is suicide. Hierarchal structures become overly concerned with chains of command. Anything that slows down product development has to be cast aside."

On Management Styles:

"There are two management styles developing in high tech in the United States. One is the *encounter group* style where the manager sees himself as a cultural leader who tries to bring out the best in people, e.g., Silicon Graphics. People work hard and tend to be exceedingly loyal. The other style is a *commando* style where everything is very dictatorial; Cabletron is a prime example. You have to be able to scream back at the boss."

On Sustaining Growth:

"The absolutely key thing to sustaining growth and profitability is mind share—establishing yourself as a player. Otherwise you get lost in the noise. You want to be in a new market niche when it becomes news. You want to be Amazon.com. In an established niche it's market differentiation—creating a case for your product. For instance, when the market becomes standardized you can differentiate on customer support and brand name."

(continued)

EXPERT OPINION (Continued)

On Innovation:

"The trick isn't so much innovation but turning the idea into a product that can be commoditized. The question to ask is, does the infrastructure exist for this technology to become wildly popular? Innovation was the browser; infrastructure was the desktop PC. The quickest way for a start-up to go out of business is to miss the point of commoditization, come in too soon and run out of cash, or come in too late to be a major player."

On Mind Share:

"Good PR needs to be built into an organization. WebTV sold a nonsaleable product to Microsoft for half a billion dollars. That's a classic case of mind share."

On Customers:

"Listen to what people are saying, and not just people who are into what you're doing. When you bring something to market for beta or alpha test, listen to the feedback and learn whether you have a product or not. You need different viewpoints and personalities to figure out if you have a product."

On Corporate Culture:

"The most important thing is to create a culture that's not bound by fear, where people feel they can make a difference. You want the kind of culture that visualizes change as growth even though sometimes that's painful. Don't fill the whole company with homogeneous personalities."

that further undermines old-fashioned hierarchy and authority. "Gen-Xers grew up in a world in which even industrial systems were run by information technologies," notes Walker Smith, managing partner at Yankelovich Partners in Norwalk, Connecticut, and coauthor of *Rocking the Ages,* a book about different generations. "When Xers look at technologies as business, they see an environment in which there are a lot of individual people pursuing their own things in support of a common objective."

It's no surprise, then, that Internet companies represent the fringe of the fringe. While technology companies in general are pushing the envelope, Internet companies may be tearing it up and throwing it away. The newest incarnation of the high-tech dream, companies that provide online content, can get started on a whim—setting up a Web site is just about costless—and go under the same way. These are the true virtual companies—collections of individuals working on "cool stuff," throwing it out and getting almost instantaneous feedback, then refining it on the fly. Making money is almost an afterthought; indeed, the Internet revenue model has yet to be determined, as we will see in examining several Internet-based companies.

This book spans the gamut of emerging technology management styles, from proven successes to the new kids on the block. The processes and techniques these companies are experimenting with will at some point find their way into mainstream corporate culture and become a part of every businessperson's lexicon. When the world is changing so rapidly, doesn't it make sense to learn from those who are moving the fastest? Venture capitalist Ann Winblad draws on a baby boomer memory to make the point about what it's like to run a high-tech company today: "It's like the guy spinning the plates on Ed Sullivan—it takes enormous energy to keep all those plates up in the air." *Silicon Gold Rush* provides insights into how the leading jugglers are keeping all of those plates up in the air.

Chapter

Leading a High-Tech Juggernaut

Making the transition from a successful start-up to an established company with staying power (i.e., consistent growth, profitability, performance, and productivity) is a difficult one for companies in all business sectors. There's many a slip between start-up and sustainability. A number of fates can befall even the most promising new companies: some disappear entirely, absorbed by other, more successful competitors or just quietly fading away; some cling to backwater products; and others, with shrinking market share, strive desperately to reinvent themselves. I've seen more than one company in a death spiral, losing its best people, unable to fill key positions, and finally deserted by customers and suppliers. Venture capitalists, not known for being politically correct, have a name for these kind of companies: "the walking dead."

What does it take to avoid becoming one of the walking dead? It starts at the top: You need a leader who can adjust his or her skills to meet the needs of the company, especially as it enters that hypergrowth phase in which revenues and the number of employees are doubling or tripling every year. Usually this leader is the CEO or the founder, but in all cases his or her principles and business philosophy set the tone for the entire company. The trick is to integrate this philosophy into every corner of the organization and sustain its influence as the company continues to grow.

David Beirne, now a general partner with Benchmark Capital in Menlo Park, is an executive search consultant who's almost as well known as his clients. They include Jim Barksdale, who Beirne recruited from Federal Express to run Netscape Communications, and Eric Schmidt, recruited from Sun Microsystems to turn Novell around. "We've always thought our job was to help the company bring in people who don't hit the Peter Principle (reaching the limits of their capability) the first day on the job," Beirne says. "The problem with the technology industry is that it's been built by a bunch of really smart people who had a vision that engulfed them. They didn't have the management talent to see above the fray."

In the typical start-up, the top person wears multiple hats: CEO, president, founder, possibly even chairman (though a venture capital backer might want to reserve that title for one of its partners). In this book, the designation "CEO" is used with the understanding that it could encompass other job titles as well. Managing a company of 20 people or so, the start-up CEO does whatever needs to get done—from answering the phone to soothing an overworked engineer, to evangelizing the company to potential customers and investors. As the company evolves, the role of CEO involves less of being the chief cook and bottle-washer and more of being the visionary dreammaker. "If the leader isn't outstanding, nothing else works," says Igor Sill, a veteran headhunter with San Francisco–based Geneva Group International. "The leader must have passion and vision and the ability to convey that vision directly to the team: Who are we, what are we doing, and how will we do it?"

"If the leader isn't outstanding, nothing else works."
—Igor Sill, Executive Search Consultant,
Geneva Group International

The CEO is vital to any company, of course, but in high tech he or she has exceptionally important external and internal roles: the first, as a public spokesperson, and the second, as a dream-maker. Unlike most consumer products, technology products are difficult to describe in accessible terms. It's the CEO who provides a human dimension to advanced technologies like databases, routers, and servers. In addition, it's usually the CEO who keeps the ideals of the company alive—for employees, investors, customers, and partners. The founder, who often assumes the mantle of CEO, is ideally suited for this. In fact, some of the most spectacularly successful high-tech companies are still guided by their founder, including Microsoft (Bill Gates), Sun Microsystems (Scott McNealy), Adobe Systems (John Warnock), and Oracle (Larry Ellison). "If you can grow the CEO from the founder, you're much better off," says venture capitalist Ann Winblad. "It's easy to buy management experience but hard to buy vision."

With visionary leadership in place, it is crucial that the founder/CEO hire a strong executive team to build on his or her strengths and add competencies of their own. This is why Bill Gates has Steve Ballmer and the rest of the vaunted Microsoft management team; why Larry Ellison has Ray Lane; why John Warnock has Charles Geschke; and why Scott McNealy has Ed Zander. The CEO must be willing not only to delegate, but to recognize and accede to superior talent in specific areas. "The two biggest issues for a CEO building a company are related," notes Steve Mader, managing director of Christian & Timbers, Boston-based national executive search consultants. "The first is finding talent. The second is realizing that, with companies growing 50 to 100 percent a year, you can't do everything personally."

The successful CEO learns how to delegate those responsibilities which do not relate to his or her evolving role in the company. As the company grows, the CEO must focus only on what *must* be done to ensure the continued success of the company. "Growth is a process of loss of control," says consultant and author Geoffrey James. "The CEO has to give responsibility and authority away." He points to CEOs like Mitchell Kertzman of Powersoft, now part of Sybase, and Lew Platt of Hewlett-Packard, who "manage the white spaces in between everyone else."

Redefining one's role within the company is a complex adjustment that not every CEO can make. Once the company reaches a certain mass, "there's no room for an autocratic individual who calls all the shots," says venture capitalist Jim Breyer of Accel Partners. "The CEO has to accept that there will be a mix of very strong, unique personalities in the management team. A balanced management team is better able to tolerate risk and experimentation." In addition, with such an emphasis on strategic dealmaking and partnering in the industry today, a diverse management team is crucial because it gives a company more opportunities to make those deals and a stronger platform to close them.

"The two biggest issues for a CEO building a company are related. The first is finding talent. The second is realizing that, with companies growing 50 to 100 percent a year, you can't do everything personally."
—Steve Mader, Managing Director, Christian & Timbers

Two young founder/CEOs who are dealing with these issues of control and delegation are Nicholas Grouf of Firefly Network, an Internet company, and Ori Sasson of Scopus Technology, a business software company. In the next few sections we'll examine how these entrepreneurs are leading their companies, given the importance of distributed management.

■ FIRING UP THE NET

Nicholas A. "Nick" Grouf was 27 years old in March 1995 when he founded Firefly, based in Cambridge, Massachusetts. His eclectic background includes business degrees from Harvard and Yale, a year in New York writing music and trying in vain to land a recording deal, and two years as a business analyst at the consulting firm McKinsey & Company. "What I loved about the process of writing music was reaching inside and articulating something I couldn't do any other way," says Grouf. The experience also "forced me to get off the treadmill and support myself in a very different fashion from what I was used to."

That background, as it happened, also came in handy while trying to give Firefly wings. Like many a founder, Grouf had to convince the world his company had a reason for being. Originally named Agents Inc. to exploit so-called intelligent agent software developed by Pattie Maes, a professor at Massachusetts Institute of Technology, the company found itself a bit ahead of the adoption curve. "When we began, there was no marketplace. In fact, there was a strong belief that technology like this wouldn't work," Grouf recalls. So he started a Web site to prove it would. (In the process, the company changed its name from Agents Inc. to the more whimsical and appealing Firefly.) The idea of an intelligent agent is that it can understand your likes and dislikes, and do such tasks as searching the Web or combing a company database for material you want.

Firefly develops software that allows electronic commerce vendors to understand who their customers are and how to approach them. Firefly's site is a good example of how to use agent software to engage customers. A reflection of Grouf's interests, the site is devoted to popular music: Visitors are asked to rate various musical artists so the agent software can assess their preferences. It can then generate a list of recommendations of other artists the visitor might like, based on its accumulated data from people with similar preferences. Firefly is now using the music site and a similar one on movies to evangelize a new market that it has dubbed "relationship management." Recognizing that agent software has a dark side—in that it can learn more about you than you might be comfortable with—Firefly has also become a champion of privacy and informed consent on the Web. "If I'm on the Web, I need to feel I'm safe and operating in an environment where I have control," Grouf says. "We're saying you don't need people's names and addresses to offer personalized service."

With Firefly employing about 80 people and growing, Grouf is eager to hire experienced managers and is recruiting veterans in such positions as finance, engineering, and sales. One of those recently hired is David Ritter, the vice president of engineering, who has been in the industry for almost two decades. "This is an organization where there's a cohesive vision of where we want to go," he says, crediting Grouf with establishing that. "He has also done the right thing in putting an expert operations team in place."

Grouf feels that he's the right CEO for now. "One of the best things about working in a consulting company like McKinsey is that you learn from other people's mistakes," he says. "It was a phenomenal education for someone who's only 22 years old." Consequently, he says, "I am where I am at Firefly not because I founded the company but because it's the opinion of the board that I am the right person for the job. If either I or they change that opinion, I will not be CEO. I think I'll be able to identify that long before they do. I have no ego issues wrapped up here as far as my title or position."

Grouf continues to define his company's role in shaping the Internet as a medium for the mass consumer market. Firefly has acquired a few high-profile clients such as America Online and Barnes & Noble Online. It is a testament to Grouf's vision and management strategy that Firefly has raised $18 million in venture capital. Grouf has exhibited several qualities required for a successful high-tech CEO, and is looking to sustain the company's growth and profitability, proving that he has the organizational ability to manage a growing company and the vision to connect a disparate team. Or it could be that he's destined to relinquish his role as CEO to a more experienced leader in the mold of other Internet companies such as Yahoo! and Netscape. If this is the case, such a transition would need to happen quickly in order to keep Firefly on its growth track. As with everything else in high tech, the problem of succession asserts itself more quickly than in traditional companies.*

■ THE ADVERSITY FACTOR

Immigrants like Andy Grove of Intel Corporation or Charles Wang of Computer Associates International have figured prominently in shaping the technology industry as we know it today. They fled bloodshed and turmoil in their own countries (Hungary and China, respectively), which may have helped prepare them for the rigors of being CEO in a competitive, high-profile industry like technology. Ori Sasson comes from a similar background. Now president and CEO of Scopus Technology of Emeryville, California, Sasson cofounded the software company with his three brothers in 1991.

Sasson's family, Iranian Jews, were forced to flee Iran when the Shah was deposed in 1979. As children there, Ori and his brothers had to duck for cover under their bed one day to avoid the errant bullets of troops who discharged their machine guns in front of the Sassons' apartment building. The family settled in Israel; Sasson and his brothers subsequently were sent to England for an education and, from there, emigrated to the United States. Sas-

---

*In April 1998, Microsoft agreed to acquire Firefly for a reported $40 million.

son attended the University of California at Berkeley, where he earned engineering and computer science degrees. He then founded Scopus after working at Hewlett-Packard and Sybase. Scopus was an early developer of software that helps businesses handle "customer care," including call center, customer support, quality assurance, and internal help desk applications.

One brother holds the position of vice president of sales, and Ori has remained at the helm of Scopus, which went public in 1995. In 1997, Scopus hit $100 million in revenues. "I am learning on the job," Sasson says. "I certainly understand that as the company grows through different stages, I'll have different responsibilities. I've taken myself out of the day-to-day operations as much as possible." Sasson, who is the prototypical visionary CEO, spoke with me on a hasty drive to nearby Oakland Airport. While clearly driven to make Scopus an even greater success (it has enjoyed 23 quarters of uninterrupted profitability, and doubled revenues every year since its founding), Sasson is surprisingly modest.

"I try to make sure my ego doesn't get in the way of making the right decision," he says. "The Scopus way is not to take yourself too seriously. We learn from mistakes and don't punish people for trying. If you're an engineer or salesperson, the organizational structure is viewed as supporting you. We're there to make them successful. I hired one person from a competitor who said they're not supposed to speak to the executive level unless spoken to. It doesn't work that way here."

Executives at Scopus, senior to Sasson in years and experience, describe him as an avid student of managerial tactics. "Over the last two years I've seen tremendous growth in Ori's maturity as a leader," says Jeffrey Bork, senior vice president of worldwide marketing. "He started this company in his late twenties; it was his first major management job. He was lacking some of the skills you would find in a CEO in a larger company. But he recognizes that he doesn't know everything he needs to, so he goes out and learns." Sasson deliberately hires people who are more experienced than he is and gives them the freedom to do the jobs they've been hired to do. According to Bork, "Once you've earned Ori's trust by showing him you can deliver, he gets out of the way and doesn't meddle. A lot of CEOs can't grow with the company; they feel they have to be part of every decision. Ori has shown the ability to step in only when necessary."

Michele L. Axelson, senior vice president and chief financial officer, was a longtime consultant at Arthur Andersen LLP before joining Scopus in 1996. "I spent 18 years in this industry watching it from the outside," she says. "It fascinated me to see the environments that had phenomenal opportunity for sustained growth. I thought I'd like to be part of something like that." She admits that she had doubts about her young CEO when she came to Scopus. "I didn't have a lot of confidence in his ability to run the company," she recalls of the period when it shot into the public eye after the initial public offering (IPO).

"A lot of CEOs can't grow with the company; they feel they have to be part of every decision. Ori has shown the ability to step in only when necessary."
—Jeffrey Bork, Senior Vice President of Worldwide Marketing, Scopus

---

The IPO may have come a little early, Axelson feels. "There was still a question of whether this was a family-owned business or a public company. There were questions about Ori's ability to communicate with financial analysts. He is not a marketeer. I knew he had a lot of work to do to articulate the strategy." Sasson worked hard to gain confidence in public speaking and honed his skills for conference presentations. Now, during meetings with Wall Street backers, "I handle the financial piece and he does the technology and product pieces," she says. "Many CEOs want to dominate everything, but he'll just smile and say, 'Michele will answer that question.' "

Grouf and Sasson are examples of CEOs who recognize their limits and are willing to do something about them. In both cases, they hired more experienced people to fill other executive positions such as marketing and sales. Grouf and Sasson were also willing to listen and learn, and prepare themselves for whatever transition their companies would make. And they gracefully acceded to change when it came. In March 1998, Scopus was acquired by Siebel Systems (see Chapter 5) for about $460 million in stock. The following month, Microsoft scooped up privately held Firefly for a reported $40 million. Such mergers are typical of the technology industry, as we'll see in Chapter 9, and are regarded by investors in the companies as a successful exit strategy, though it's not always an easy transition for the founder to turn over his "baby" to a new parent.

■ BRINGING IN NEW BLOOD

If a CEO's leadership style is focused on one aspect or function of the company, the culture of the company follows suit—perhaps to the detriment of the company as a whole. According to David R. Mather, managing director in Cupertino, California, for the national search firm Christian & Timbers, "Everybody's strength, if you take it too far, becomes a weakness." That's why the CEO of a growing company must have a balance of skills and be willing to acquire individuals who add more strengths to the mix. While founder/CEOs are successful in part due to their risk-taking perspective and technological vision, these qualities alone cannot sustain the organization's success. Hiring an executive management team that can supply the company with more structure and focus is essential. In some cases, this may eventually mean that the CEO relinquishes his or her role to a more experienced business professional. "An astute CEO knows when he or she is out of gas for the next level," says headhunter Igor Sill.

"You can't assume that your original CEO will go all the way," says Howard Anderson, who's both a venture capitalist and an analyst of high-tech trends for The Yankee Group. "Companies need different talents at different stages of development. This is rarely an industry where the management stays constant. You need some level of matured leadership." By which he means that technology companies are often started by a group of young people whose skills are the very ones that make a start-up successful. These individuals are reckless in breaking down barriers and finding new markets.

But when the company starts shipping a product and winds up with an installed base of customers and contracts with suppliers and partnership deals with other vendors, the CEO must be more focused on their needs and less on risk-taking. This is the point where the founder or the board must decide whether to introduce new management to guide the company as it matures. The next few sections describe how two companies handled the difficult task of replacing the founding CEO.

■ A ROCKY START

Carol Bartz, the chairman and CEO of Autodesk in San Rafael, California, knows what it's like to follow in the footsteps of a founder—and an eccentric one at that. Autodesk's board of directors recruited Bartz to take the top job in 1992, a decade after John Walker founded the company and became its technical visionary. In assuming the role of CEO at Autodesk, Bartz replaced someone who wasn't ready to leave the company. Walker stayed on at Autodesk in a product development position. In addition to this problematic transition, Bartz had to face two difficult personal challenges. As the first woman to be recruited from the outside to head a major technology company, she was the subject of massive press scrutiny. And, about a week after accepting the position, Bartz learned that she had breast cancer. She had to speak openly about the diagnosis because of disclosure requirements for publicly traded companies.

Bartz had exhibited the sophistication and maturity needed to handle the CEO's spot after serving in top management positions at Sun Microsystems and Digital Equipment, but she had never managed an entire company before—and Autodesk was hardly a smooth-running organization. The leader in CAD software, Autodesk at the time of Bartz's ascendancy had almost no formal structure for handling such vital functions as product development, employee compensation, or human resources. The culture was molded around the whims of its brilliant programmers, chiefly Walker, who made decisions to pursue interesting projects without regard for marketability or profitability. Walker remained part of the company for a time as a programmer, although he moved to Switzerland, leaving officially in 1994.

Bartz's previous managerial stints had brought her from the East Coast to the West Coast, and to a new view of corporate purpose. "When I came to Silicon Valley with Sun," she says, "I realized the mission was not to protect what you had, as it had been on the East Coast. The mission in the Valley is to view yourself as the competition. It isn't about what we have, it's about where we can be." That was "an incredible mind switch," Bartz recalls. "You learn quickly how to manage that process of looking toward the future, as opposed to wringing your hands about what happened yesterday."

"It isn't about what we have, it's about where we can be."
—Carol Bartz, CEO, Autodesk

Today, five years after Bartz stepped in as Autodesk's CEO, transition to a functional organization is complete.

As a $600 million company, it is the fifth-largest in the PC software industry. Autodesk is clearly Bartz's organization now, and the company's early culture and sensibilities have matured and been transformed under her leadership. Bartz has brought in a new management team, acquired some companies and sold others, established an infrastructure and a schedule for developing and shipping new products, and made numerous agreements with new business partners.

Steve McMahon is vice president of human resources for Autodesk. "When I first came the company was very founder-driven—iconoclastic, no organizational structure, in love with technology," says McMahon. "The vision of the technology was what got people excited. Carol came in with more professional management. People complain that it's getting too bureaucratic, not as much fun, but I ask them, 'Do you want to learn how to brush your teeth again?' We have grown up. There's accountability and goals and objectives." And Bartz has been the primary agent for that change.

■ A SMOOTH SUCCESSION

Autodesk is an example of a company where the founder had to be eased out. This is not the case with Open Market, where the founder welcomed his successor with open arms. In fact, four-year-old Open Market of Burlington, Massachusetts, is a textbook example of how to handle the transition to a new CEO. (Older companies take note.) The handoff was seamless because Open Market's founder and original CEO, Shikhar Ghosh, remains a very active chairman. Ghosh retains his role as visionary, while complementing that with the more pragmatic skills of Gary Eichhorn as president, CEO, and day-to-day manager. Ghosh himself recruited Eichhorn, who had led two Massachusetts-based Hewlett-Packard operations: workstations and medical products. The two men respect each other and know each other's limits and strengths. There is no sense of rancor or displacement between them. The transition was eased because Ghosh's change in position was voluntary rather than one mandated by the board.

Eichhorn joined the firm in late 1995, when Open Market was transitioning from a consulting practice to a products company distributing software that enables Internet commerce. Says Ghosh: "I wasn't really looking for a CEO when I met Gary." Ghosh believed he had the skills to grow Open Market himself because he had managed another entrepreneurial company, Appex Corporation, from 1988 to 1994 and had also operated a large division at Electronic Data Systems (EDS). "Gary came here as an HP customer with a particular problem," Ghosh recalls. "He and I wound up spending three to four hours talking about Open Market and what we could do. Where we really connected was an overall feeling of what the company should be." That was to move away from consulting and into licensing software.

Seizing the moment, Ghosh decided that he and Eichhorn together would provide stronger leadership for Open Market than he could alone. Previously a partner with the Boston Consulting Group, Ghosh takes a big-picture approach to running the business, while Eichhorn focuses more on financial and operational results. "If you take it to extremes, I would be a consultant and he'd be a manufacturing head," Ghosh adds. "I don't consider constraints. Gary does. He is very good at taking a large group of people and getting them all channeled. He can prioritize their goals and put together an operational structure to make things happen." That leaves Ghosh free to focus on longer-term issues such as collaborating with partners and assessing potential acquisitions.

Once Ghosh and the board had made the decision to hire Eichhorn, Ghosh deliberately moved away from operational managing, signaling to employees who was in charge. "In the first eight months after Gary came, I didn't attend a single management meeting," Ghosh says. "I knew it would be impossible for Gary if I was always there. Then how do you know who's really running the show?" Letting go, says Ghosh, "was emotionally hard for me to do. At the point that Gary came aboard, I had hired everyone in the company. But it was clear to me that Gary was going to run the company under his rules. If it didn't work out between us, I would be the one leaving."

"If you have processes that take care of the trivia, you can step back from the routine stuff and focus on things that really make a difference. What you can't do is have everybody innovate all the time because you end up with chaos."

—Shikhar Ghosh, Chairman and founder, Open Market

It was clear to Ghosh that Open Market's informal organization could not continue if the company were to continue growing at such a volatile rate. "A company with an informal structure gets run by personality," he says. "When I was making all the decisions, people would look to me all the time. But that meant you couldn't introduce complexity into the business." As Open Market approaches the $100 million mark, "we've got to have a way of managing ourselves so that the machinery works." Innovation can occur, but within areas designated by the decision framework. Ghosh believes having that framework reduces tedium. "Most of our lives are filled with trivial stuff," he says. "If you have processes that take care of the trivia, you can step back from the routine stuff and focus on things that really make a difference. What you can't do is have everybody innovate all the time because you end up with chaos."

If Open Market continues on its current growth track, Eichhorn and Ghosh could become the equivalent of such famously successful management partnerships as Oracle's

Ellison and Lane or Microsoft's Gates and Ballmer. "We both hold the baton," says Eichhorn. "It's true that I run the day-to-day operations since I'm experienced in that. But Shikhar has phenomenal vision. He understands what's happening and what's going to happen in the market. He continues to look over the horizon. He and I meet every day."

■ MATURITY VERSUS YOUTH

High-tech executives, particularly at start-ups, are often younger than their counterparts in nontech industries. Many start-up CEOs are Gen-Xers in their twenties, as exemplified by Firefly and Scopus. Even veteran executives recruited to offer professional management, like Bartz and Eichhorn, are Baby Boomers in their forties—relatively old by technology industry standards, but young in almost any other industry. "Xers are setting up companies where self-reliance and entrepreneurialism are the strongest elements, and everyone wants to be their own boss," says Walker Smith, the Yankelovich Partners' expert in generational differences. "They look to Boomers to come in and provide them with organizational guidance."

There is a generation gap when it comes to CEO attributes—which may account for some of the differences in the management style and organizational structure between tech and nontech companies, according to research by Hagberg Consulting Group of Foster City, California. Hagberg specializes in cultural and leadership assessments and over the past 14 years has collected data on and from 550 chief executives, most of whom head technology companies. Hagberg produced unique data for this book relating to CEO age and characteristics (see Appendix B). Performance ratings indicate that CEO attributes of persuasiveness, risk-taking, decisiveness, and creativity are all perceived to decrease with age. In contrast, thoroughness, open-mindedness, facilitation of teamwork, sensitivity, listening, short-term planning, and subordinate involvement are thought to increase with age. When CEOs rate themselves, they see impulsiveness, abasement, liveliness, apprehension, and vigilance decreasing with age, and conformity and even-temperedness increasing with age.

"Older executives learn from experience; they're not such cowboys," says Hagberg senior consultant Ellen Shuck. "They have learned to put other priorities in their lives besides just work and they have learned how to interact with other people. They're more willing to delegate, but they're also thorough in following through to make sure something gets done." Applying this to the companies we've profiled here, Grouf and Sasson fit the descriptions of young, entrepreneurial CEOs: They're impulsive and eager, but sometimes disorganized and tentative. The older Eichhorn and Bartz have seen and done more, so they're better able to assess their company's current needs—but may not be as willing as the other two to leap into the unknown.

"Older executives learn from experience; they're not such cowboys."
—Ellen Shuck, Senior Consultant, Hagberg Consulting Group

For purposes of this book, Hagberg also broke down the CEO self-assessments by large versus small companies (the dividing line was $300 million in annual revenues). In contrast with small-company CEOs, large-company leaders are more aggressive in pursuing goals, more structured and process-oriented, much more concerned with status and recognition, more trusting, more accepting, more patient, more time-pressured, and more dominant about getting their way. They also tend to get less satisfaction from work, take fewer risks, and are less independent. (See Appendix B.)

CEOs WHO ARE MAKING THE GRADE

By Mary Pat McCarthy, Partner and National Director, Software and Services, and Edwin Rodriguez, Partner and National Director, Electronics, KPMG Peat Marwick LLP, Palo Alto, California.

Top Marks for CEOs:

Eric Benhamou of 3Com

➤ A bold risk-taker.

➤ Gained tremendous mind share.

➤ Skilled at choosing and integrating strategic partners.

Cheryl Vedoe of 10th Planet

➤ Has a keen strategic focus.

➤ Cultivates a strong corporate identity and market dominance.

➤ Exhibits strong team-building and people skills.

Dave Duffield of PeopleSoft

➤ Exhibits a strong leadership and nurturing management style.

➤ Has a keen strategic focus.

➤ Aligned corporate vision with company's goals and operations.

(continued)

CEOs WHO ARE MAKING THE GRADE
(Continued)

Tim Koogle of Yahoo!

➤ Is a strong team builder.

➤ Created a paradigm shift.

➤ Exhibits leadership skills that support self-actualization and ownership.

Tom Siebel of Siebel Systems

➤ Is the king of mind share.

➤ Maintains a keen strategic focus that is aligned with operations.

➤ Exhibits strong leadership that supports employee ownership.

Ralph Ungermann of First Virtual Corporation

➤ Exhibits strong leadership that emphasizes self-actualization and alignment.

➤ Distributes leadership throughout the company.

➤ Maintains a strong web of relationships.

■ THE BOTTOM LINE

The perfect high-tech CEO would probably be a mix of maestro, magician, messiah, and mother. You'd want qualities from all four of the individuals profiled in this chapter: Bartz's people skills and Eichhorn's calm authority and Sasson's excitement and Grouf's devotion to a cause. Headhunter David Beirne describes what he looks for in a potential CEO: "You have to be incredibly smart, have tremendous energy, and have an ability to filter huge amounts of data and decipher that information quickly."

He emphasizes that people smarts are more important than technical smarts. Great CEOs have to be able to get employees to rally around them. They like to collaborate and are usually quite extroverted. He adds that the best CEOs "are both nurturers and tough as nails, depending on what the situation calls for."

"CEOs today don't fall in love with their own decisions. If you make a decision and get a result, you're in the position to make another decision, as opposed to trying to conceptualize the whole process before you move."
—David Mather, Executive Search Consultant,
Christian & Timbers

The Soul of a New Company: The Value of Being Small

At the heart of the technology industry is a paradox: Small companies are all trying to grow bigger, while big companies are all trying to think smaller. A small company is eager to get into what Geoffrey Moore calls the "tornado" phase, where it's suddenly swept up in an explosive market, with growth rates to match. In this chapter, we'll look at the role of corporate culture at small entrepreneurial technology companies, which I define as those with annual sales less than $100 million.

"Culture" is often mistakenly thought of as a part of a company's structure rather than as an extension of its identity. As such, small companies sometimes don't even realize that they have a culture. They're just trying to get things done as quickly as possible by whoever is available. After visiting the headquarters of the 20-plus technology companies described in this book, it's clear to me that culture is actually far more important to newer companies than it is to the more traditional companies. Very often, the corporate culture at traditional companies is an outgrowth of their processes. They have executive teams and a staff that have been together, in many cases, for years. There's a sense of common history, a system of mentors, a pecking order, and procedures that provide consistency. The culture, for better or worse, is established, and changing that culture takes tremendous effort.

By contrast, entrepreneurial technology companies are most often a collection of people from diverse backgrounds banded together by a shared dream. As noted in the first chapter, no one has to stay, and no one does for very long. Except for the founders, I seldom run into people who had been at any of these companies for more than a few years. So you don't see a cadre of long-term employees who are the cultural griots—passing on the oral history and mores. At a newly assembled company, it falls upon the management team to establish a basic set of core values, and then be able to reinvent their culture on the fly as the company absorbs or merges with other companies, repositions itself in the market, or loses a key team leader. Culture becomes a deliberate creation, much like technology itself, that begins with a shared vision and gains texture as the company responds to flux in the marketplace.

Once there are too many people for everyone to have regular access to the entrepreneur/founder, the organization must develop formal structures that can either enhance its entrepreneurial culture or undermine it.

One balancing act perfected by successful technology companies is the trick of sustaining a management style and infrastructure that's both flexible enough to nurture creativity and structured enough to handle growth. And the point of balance is the corporate culture, the shared values that, stated or unstated, govern the way the company approaches its customers, treats its employees, interacts with vendors and shareholders, and handles the unexpected. Every company reaches the point when it must define itself formally. "All start-ups look alike until they're too large to get together once a week in the meeting room," says Moore. "Up to that point—about 70 employees—you can maintain the camaraderie, make decisions very quickly as a team or leave them to the individual entrepreneur." But once there are too many people for everyone to have regular access to the entrepreneur/founder, the organization must develop formal structures that can either enhance its entrepreneurial culture or undermine it.

■ SHOW ME THE MONEY

The first defining aspect of culture for a start-up is how the company was financed. If the company is bootstrapped—funded by its founder and friends, with no venture capital—it will tend to be inwardly focused and quirky. Its personality will flow from its founder/entrepreneur. I found the quintessential example of this in Tom Siebel, whose namesake company, Siebel Systems of San Mateo, California, sells sales automation software. Before starting his own company, Siebel was a consummate salesman at the notoriously hard-nosed Oracle. Siebel Systems, where even the conference rooms are named after major customers, reflects its founder's customer-oriented view of the world and his single-minded determination to be a market leader.

"There's a zeal, a courage and tenacity required for people who gravitate to start-ups," says David Powell, Sr., a longtime high-tech headhunter with offices in Woodside. "They're also greedy. Their greed is about power, control, innovation and money. They need to be leading the pack in some way."

"There's a zeal, a courage and tenacity required for peo-
ple who gravitate to start-ups."
—David Powell, Sr., Executive Search Consultant,
David Powell Inc.

A company with a lot of venture capital sunk into it
has to think about a return for its investors. Consequently
it will be more outwardly driven and generally have less
control over its future than one like Siebel. The board of
directors will be stacked with venture capitalists who
won't hesitate to oust the founder if they think that person
lacks the capacity to bring the company public or to sell
it at a high value. Balancing that reality is the fact that a
venture-backed company has access to the web of relationships the venture capital firm has built up, including
other entrepreneurs, lawyers, executive search firms, consultants, and accountants, all of whom can offer advice
and support. This is the typical model of today's high-tech
start-up.

A company that has relied on the increasingly common
"angel" investor—a former entrepreneur who has become
an investor after successfully building up one or more start-
ups—may find itself adrift if its chief executive cannot
stand up to the investor and establish a separate identity for
the company. The prototypical angel is Paul Allen, an inde-
pendently wealthy cofounder of Microsoft Corporation,
who now puts his billions into funding start-ups. Ironically,
his companies (which include Starwave Corporation) have
never become marketplace powers—probably because
being so well endowed financially, they lack the hunger
that drives others whose resources are more limited. For example, Starwave, an Internet content company partly
owned by Allen, is still searching for its place in the world
after growing up with an indulgent father.

Another approach is to augment angel or venture capital with investments from strategic partners, typically

other technology companies who want to leverage their products with innovative new ones. These strategic partners come with their own baggage—they want something from the start-up, like linkage to an exciting new product or entree to a new market or a potential acquisition. Sometimes the demands are conflicting, and the burden falls on the start-up to retain its focus despite its partners' squabbles. What pulls the strings is where the resources are coming from, and companies can get pulled in a lot of different ways by partners. General Magic, of Mountain View, was spun off from Apple Computer in 1990 with the intent of developing an operating system for mobile computing devices. It raised an estimated $77 million from such high-powered backers as Apple, AT&T, Sony, and Motorola, but never managed to follow through on its vision. In part, General Magic was stymied because all its partners had competing aims, and it is now trying to reposition itself as an Internet company.

To deliver any type of return to investors, the start-up must identify and exploit its value to customers and to the industry. Historically, venture investors looked for an overall rate of return return of 18 to 22 percent on a fund that backed a number of companies. These returns are usually achieved via initial public offerings and acquisitions of the portfolio companies. Today, expectations have been raised by the performance of such companies as Yahoo!, Amazon.com, and Ciena, whose tremendous success in the public market gave investors triple-digit returns. "Companies try to accurately define the streams of knowledge they're going to attempt to navigate, and align themselves with that," says Raymond Miles, professor of organizational behavior at the University of California at Berkeley and former dean of its School of Business. "There are very high margins associated with being at the front end of the stream." To a certain extent, defining that stream means defining your culture. If it's a very fast-moving stream with lots of currents, like Internet content, you need extreme tolerance of risk and resilience from mistakes. If it's a small stream with the potential to be-come a huge river, like networking was when Cisco Sys-tems started out, you need a solid infrastructure to which others can hold fast in the flood. If it's a relative backwater, like educational software, you need genuine commitment and devotion to a different ideal than becoming a billion-dollar enterprise.

Says Miles: "You have to model yourself like the envi-ronments you're facing. People get frightened in the midst of enormous complexity, but you have to design an orga-nization that's as complex as the arena in which you're op-erating. If you try to simplify your structure, that means simplifying the world you're looking at, focusing only on some of the pieces."

Now let's look at how some specific companies are modeling themselves.

"You have to model yourself like the environments you're facing."
—Raymond Miles, Professor of Organizational Behavior,
University of California at Berkeley

■ GREAT EXPECTATIONS

CrossWorlds' Katrina Garnett, who we met in the last chap-ter, is one of the most intense people I've seen in the tech-nology industry. Garnett's profile would fit right in with the twenty-first-century superwoman who insists on hav-ing it all—she makes Xena the Warrior Princess look like a lightweight. When I interviewed Garnett in the summer of 1997 she was running a start-up technology company, preparing for a product launch, raising one child and get-ting ready to deliver her second in a few months, heading a foundation devoted to improving girls' interest in sci-ence and math, and writing a book about founding a company. Despite all these pressures, it is clear that she takes the time to care about her employees, many of whom devotedly followed her to CrossWorlds from previous companies before they even knew what the new one was going to be doing. Garnett obviously pays attention to not just what she wants to do, but how she wants to do it. The launch party described in Chapter 1 was orchestrated and implemented by her, right down to the guest list.

Australian by birth, Garnett has been in California for 12 years and speaks with little trace of an accent. She calls herself "second-generation high-tech"; her father worked for Data General Corporation, one of the old-line minicomputer manufacturers that faded when the personal computer took over. Perhaps because she's seen how quickly shifts in technology can leave a company behind, Garnett is determined to do whatever it takes to succeed. She's careful to craft the right image, spending long hours polishing her speech for the product launch and declining the offer of a major business magazine that wanted to pose her in a bubble bath to illustrate its list of 20 cool companies. "No one would take me seriously after that," she says. (Contrast that with the founder of Cisco, Sandy Lerner, who perched naked on top of a horse for *Forbes* magazine.)

Most companies, says Garnett, "are like aimless ships sailing around because the people on board don't know where they're headed." At CrossWorlds, every new hire gets a copy of the business plan with strategy, product dates, and deadlines. She measures the company's growth by how many pizzas it takes to feed everyone at weekly all-hands meetings: "We were a two-pizza company; now [with more than 60 employees] we're a ten-pizza company." Garnett tries to tell her employees as much as possible, even the bad news, like what happens if an important investor pulls out. "I don't sit on that kind of information. My door is always open. I do whatever it takes to over-communicate."

Among the high-tech CEOs who invested personally in CrossWorlds are Michael Dell of Dell Computer Corporation and Dave Duffield of PeopleSoft. With all that venture capital and investment from her peers, Garnett bears a heavy load of expectation on her shoulders. "Our first priority," she says, "is getting the product out. We still have to prove ourselves by delivering." To that end, she has established a product development process with specific timetables and performance benchmarks, such as the ability to connect to products made by CrossWorlds' partners.

To prepare for growth, Garnett's formula is to hire managers and engineers who are impatient with the status quo and eager to move up and tackle even more challenges. In technology, the speed at which the industry and your competitors are moving forces you to hire quickly—and sometimes fire quickly, if you've made a mistake. Scott Martin, senior vice president of sales and service, joined in late 1996. "I talked to Katrina on Tuesday and had an offer letter on Thursday. I accepted on Friday and started on the following Monday," he recalls. Garnett says that one vice president was let go after two months because "he wasn't having the impact I expected; he wasn't pulling his weight. I could look like a weak manager if I didn't deal with it."

In stark comparison to staunchly traditional companies, technology start-ups like CrossWorlds don't have well-defined positions that match neatly with the job skills that are listed on someone's resume. Instead, they go after people whose personalities are in sync with the culture and goals that the company has established. This makes hiring, at least in the early stages, a somewhat subjective and arbitrary process. It's no accident that several of the premier technology companies, like Microsoft and Sun Microsystems, were comprised of individuals who graduated from college together. Picking up on this model, Garnett was able to find employees who shared her sensibilities by recruiting liberally from her former companies.

But CrossWorlds' culture is not just a reflection of its founder's background. Garnett prefers to give people latitude in shaping their environment and making decisions—jumping in only when something isn't getting done. She has been an engineer, product manager, and executive, so little escapes her. "She'll notice when something's not right personally and ask about it," says Mike Donaldson, vice president of marketing and a longtime friend. He worked with Garnett for six years at her previous company, Sybase, before joining her at CrossWorlds. "She tells you what she wants, and when she's not happy. There's always a time-line in her head for when a decision should be made."

Garnett is a self-described people person who, on this level at least, fits the stereotype of a female executive. "I'm very nurturing," she acknowledges. "People want to be listened to." She encourages managers to have one-on-one meetings with employees. "People need daily feedback. That way nothing has time to fester. You deal with problems on a real-time basis." She also believes in allowing people to grow. CrossWorlds, small as it is, will pay for training and development seminars. "As long as people feel like they're learning, they're much happier," Garnett says. "I myself get bored every six months. I always push myself to do something new."

"People need daily feedback. That way nothing has time to fester. You deal with problems on a real-time basis."
—Katrina Garnett, CEO, CrossWorlds

Garnett is one of those executives who runs the risk of spreading herself too thin. "The challenge with Katrina is that she has so much going on in her head, you have to interpret what's coming out," says Donaldson. To be a completely successful entrepreneur, Garnett will have to focus by zeroing in on one step at a time, like product development or assembling a team. She might need to modify her company's culture in the direction of Intel, which, while it may not be the most comfortable or nurturing place to work, usually gets its products out as promised.

■ THE WILL TO WIN

The corporate personality at Visigenic Software of San Mateo resembles a combination of linebacker and social worker—tough as nails, yet paternalistic. This seeming contradiction harks back almost a quarter-century to when Visigenic founder and CEO Roger Sippl was a nineteen-year-old premed student at the University of California at Berkeley and was diagnosed with Hodgkin's disease. "I was supposed to die," he remembers. "They told me I had a 20 percent chance of living." Fortunately for Sippl, his background gave him the ability to find out the best possible experimental treatment, which, as it turned out, was being done just down the freeway at Stanford University.

Though he has never had a relapse, the brush with death left its mark. For one thing, Sippl had to switch majors to computer science after realizing "they weren't going to let me into medical school because they were afraid I might die on them." He had to stay in school to keep his university-funded health benefits, which paid for the treatments. "I threw up for a year, but I stayed in school," he says. The experience engendered a determination to win at all costs. "After the Hodgkin's disease, everything I did had to be highly optimized to survive. That overflowed every move I made. I optimize for enterprise success, not financial return or comfort. I always tell the employees, your mind-set has to be to win, not build the coolest product or get the most shares [of stock]."

Sippl has founded three technology companies, of which the first, Informix Software, has been the most successful by far. Informix, now one of the top three players in the important field of database software, also made Sippl's personal fortune. Sippl's history impacted Visigenic by engendering a culture that is top-down and personality-driven. Sippl personifies the expression "still waters run deep." With his controlled demeanor and mild expression, he does not fit the traditional description of a driven entrepreneur. Bob Macdonald, Visigenic's vice president of marketing, has known Sippl since high school, when they were in jazz band together. "Roger's biggest strength—some would call it a weakness—is his single-mindedness in pursuing something," Macdonald says. "That enables him to think through an issue thoroughly. He's famous for missing the exit on the freeway because he's deep in thought." Visigenic is a result of Sippl's effort to bore down into a narrow, but hopefully deep, niche market: The company's software product is called an object request broker (ORB), which allows applications on different machines to exchange information. ORBs are used by corporate programmers to develop information systems.

At Visigenic, Sippl is "always focused on business. His companies are characterized by being driven by business needs, not employee needs," Macdonald says. At Informix, "he had everybody wear coats and ties, including the programmers, because he wanted to say to people that this was a business application company."

Sippl is willing to delegate responsibilities. "He has an appreciation for details, but he realizes other people can be better at it," says Macdonald. "What he went through when he got cancer forced him to think through his priorities." But Sippl is clearly the person at Visigenic who makes the key decisions. "Consensus-driven" and "empowerment" are not adjectives that apply to his company. "Now that we've figured out our market and value proposition, it's time for everybody to fall in line and we'll charge up the hill," he says, sounding a bit like Apple's Steve Jobs. In the technology industry of the 1990s, Sippl adds, "there's always some billion-dollar company you have to outengineer and outmarket. You don't have time to mess about with a company poll." Taking the place of its currently leased headquarters, Sippl wants to erect a new structure for Visigenic that includes a multi-tier theater "where I can gather everyone comfortably in a room and have them see and hear me."

Since my meeting with Sippl, Visigenic has been acquired by Borland International, a much larger software company. In April 1998, Borland changed its name to Inprise Corporation. Visigenic's fate—that of being swallowed by another company—demonstrates the limits inherent in an organization that is based on a lone individual and a niche technology with limited growth potential. To be too single-minded means missing the forest because you've concentrated on a tree.

■ THE HP WANNABE

In the first chapter, I described the Hewlett-Packard Company as one of the primary reference points of high-technology culture. Nowhere is that more evident than at Open Market. Can you see the culture clash coming? With Internet companies, the adjectives that come to mind are "freewheeling," "youthful," and "high-spirited." With HP, it's "veteran," "consensus-minded," and "respectful." So how has Open Market been able to combine such disparate influences? The answer is key to how a maturing technology company can maintain a culture that encourages innovation and excitement.

Originally venture capital–funded and now publicly traded, Open Market started in 1994 as a business-to-business company offering consulting services to clients who wanted to do Internet-based commerce. It later developed products to make it easier to carry out transactions on the Web. Founder Shikhar Ghosh made the crucial move that introduced elements of HP to Open Market's culture—bringing in former HP executive Gary Eichhorn as CEO. "I'm a tremendous fan of HP," says Eichhorn. "They pioneered a management style and processes that are world-class." He admits that if HP were headquartered in Boston rather than California, "I wouldn't be here." But Eichhorn was itching to run his own show, and the opportunity to do this at HP only existed on the West Coast, where he didn't want to move.

Ghosh, whose title is now chairman, remembers how some of Eichhorn's notions of company culture had to change when he came to Open Market. "I'll never forget the look on his face when I showed him his office—the same-size cubicle as everyone else's. At HP he had an office and his own conference room, and even his secretary had an office. But he said, 'If that's the culture, that's what I'll do.' " The second day of Eichhorn's tenure, one of the dogs, whom employees were accustomed to bringing to the office, "came in and peed in his cube," laughs Ghosh. "It went against every bit of HP training, but he was willing to understand our culture."

While tolerating some of Open Market's culture, Eichhorn went on to introduce numerous facets of the HP way. "The standing joke around here is to introduce new ideas with the set-up, 'The way we used to do it at HP . . .' " says Eichhorn. Outside the workplace, respect for family life, another HP tenet, is part of Open Market's culture as well. "We have a very strong belief in supporting people's families and a life outside work," stresses the CEO. "If employees need to be out to take care of their family, they're encouraged to do it. We do that because it's the right thing to do."

Of course, not everything from HP, which is a $45 billion behemoth, could be transferred directly to Open Market, which is approaching $60 million in annual sales. "I have to scale the management philosophy and style to a small enterprise," says Eichhorn. "HP gives us a foundation of processes, which some start-ups think is a dirty word. I think companies hit the wall because they don't have infrastructure in place." Since Eichhorn joined, Open Market has grown from 175 to 500 people. "I use a deliberate planning process. I want everyone to understand what's expected," he says. He has put a decision-making process in place to foster business planning and communication. "If you have a framework of things that you understand need to be done, it frees you to think of new ideas," he says. "If you do things haphazardly, you're always stuck in fire drills."

Before Eichhorn came along, says Ghosh, "we were a fly-by-the-seat-of-your-pants company." Eichhorn's decision-making framework channels innovation, Ghosh says, by "telling people who have an idea about a new product feature who to go to. This is not an organizational chart; it's a chart for how the company functions. We were bringing in lots of new people and they needed to know how they fit into the structure."

Because Open Market operates in the chaotic Internet arena and has many young employees, there are areas where its culture diverges from HP. "We do tolerate a certain amount of irreverent, unconventional behavior," says Ghosh—like bringing dogs to work or holding a periodic "trivia bowl" where contestants answer a series of questions while dressed in bathrobes and shower caps. The premise: Clothes don't matter to performance. "You allow people to have fun but you also establish what will not be tolerated," says Ghosh. "Disrespect for accounting or human resources or marketing isn't tolerated. There's the notion of respecting individuals regardless of what they do."

Eichhorn has hired for both experience and enthusiasm: "We have a very vibrant group of employees." He will accept dissension, but not yelling. "People disagree with me all the time," he says, "but there's always respect underneath the disagreement. I don't care how brilliant people are; I will not tolerate those who don't treat others with respect. Powerful teams, not individuals, make great companies."

Financially, Open Market is currently a modest success, with a solid revenue stream and growing number of large customers. Culturally, it has managed to retain a sense of individual freedom while imposing a certain amount of business discipline, thanks to a CEO who tempers his HP-based management style with the needs of an entrepreneurial company.

■ E-MAILS ACROSS THE SEA

Check Point Software Technologies, devoted to making the Internet safe for corporations, had a 10,000-mile cultural divide to bridge. In 1993, two young Israeli engineers, who had served their mandatory stint in the military there setting up and connecting computer systems, decided that the nascent World Wide Web could use some of their expertise. The explosive growth in Web use by businesses and consumers worldwide also meant increasing opportunity for break-ins and illicit use of information. Gil Schwed and Shlomo Kramer, joined a few months later by Marius Nacht, set out to create software—called a firewall—that would protect corporate Web sites by filtering out unwanted entrants.

But Check Point had a problem shared by many international companies: It was strong on technology but lacked the marketing sophistication and clout needed to penetrate the U.S. market. So the founders set up a U.S. subsidiary in Redwood City, California, Check Point Software Technologies, and recruited Deb Triant, formerly vice president of marketing at desktop publishing giant Adobe Systems, as CEO and president. With her shoulder-length blonde hair, girl-next-door looks, and outgoing manner, Triant seems like she should be one of the wholesome "let's-put-on-a-show" kids in those old Judy Garland/ Mickey Rooney movies. Her role at Check Point is twofold: On the strategy side, she is the marketing expert, and on the cultural side, she is the "mom" who deals with squabbles and misunderstandings.

A mother in real life, Triant brings her nurturing skills to her company, where melding the clashing cultures of unconventional Silicon Valley with harder-edged, Israeli business determination takes considerable patience and tact. Jackie Ross, Check Point's vice president of marketing, can attest to her CEO's sensitivity to the human element. Ross recalls that shortly after she joined the company in mid-1996, "I was going through a very challenging time because of all our growth and everything we were trying to do in marketing." Triant returned from a trip and asked Ross for an update. "I started to tell her what was going on, and she said, 'I'm looking at your face and I see some stress. Why don't you come over to my house and I'll even cook for you.'" She fixed margaritas and snacks, and the two sat on the patio and talked. Says Ross: "I got the sense that this is someone who cares about me, even when everybody is running fast. You put so much of yourself into it that to feel appreciation of yourself as an individual is very important."

On a larger scale, Triant's nurturing abilities enable her to accommodate "two cultural elements pulling in very different ways." Many of the Israel-based employees came out of the military, where communication is confined to "There's your job, go do it." But in the United States, technology company employees are accustomed to lots of dialogue and team interaction in figuring out who does what. As a result, "In the early days there were some real flames [angry e-mail messages] going across the ocean," recalls Triant. "Over here, people feel they have a right to e-mail the CEO or anyone else. They tell me, 'You shouldn't have done that.' Over there that kind of e-mail is misinterpreted as a lack of respect." Triant finally sent out an e-mail directive of her own, telling people not to get too wound up if they got an e-mail with emotional content. Don't just keep the flame going; call the person, she suggested, and have a conversation in real time. Sometimes programmers forget how to do that.

When I talked to a couple of Israeli engineers who are working in Check Point's U.S. headquarters, their responses to my questions were typically blunt, direct, and unadorned. I've been to Israel to cover its thriving technology industry and have found that while Israelis can be painfully honest, they don't give you the soap opera–type confidences we've come to expect from American-style interviews. So I wasn't too surprised when the two engineers shrugged off questions about corporate culture as irrelevant. Their interest was in their work. "Here [in the United States] all the people are money-driven and in Israel they are not," said one of the engineers, Nir Zak, manager of application development. "Here the mood of the people is very correlated to the price of the stock. In Israel they don't really care. They want to do their job."

Triant realized that e-mail alone wasn't going to solve the cultural problems. When you're talking about people getting along with people, technology can't replace face-to-face interaction. Among Check Point's workforce of 180 people, half are employed in Israel and half in the United States, with most at the two locations never having met. So in the summer of 1997 the company took a large group of employees from both countries, along with their spouses, to Spain for five days. "The majority of time was just vacationing, but we squeezed in a few business meetings to talk about new products and channels," says Triant. The real goal was just to get people comfortable with each other. Based on the heightened camaraderie that developed at the Spain meeting, she was already planning to take her management staff to Israel for a strategy meeting the following year.

Check Point, which went public in 1996 and had revenues of $80 million in 1997, is on the cusp of becoming a big company, so Triant knows she's got to put some structures in place to support the coming growth. Beyond the cultural differences caused by having two such geographically dispersed headquarters, "there's a lot of natural friction, tension, and stress caused by high growth," she says. "Jobs are not well defined. There's an awful lot of 'I thought you were going to do that.' " On the other hand, because of the nature of the work and the people who do it, no one wants anything rigid or bureaucratic. "Programmers are like cats," Triant confides. "They can't be herded." So Check Point develops formal processes by exception. Says Triant, "Whenever we put a structure in place, we ask ourselves, What would be the consequences if we don't do it? Will there be serious problems? If the answer is no, we don't do it. We don't want to put our energy into something that's not going to pay back."

So, only about 20 percent of what goes on at Check Point has been formalized, Triant figures, and these are limited to the most essential functions. For example, given the separation of staff, good communications were imperative, so the company started an internal newsletter and Web site. There have to be performance reviews so that people can get raises and promotions—but the manager only has to fill out a two- or three-page form evaluating strengths and weaknesses, and goals to work on. The questions are open-ended, like "What are the three most important things for doing this job?" The product development process has to have deadlines and goals, because Check Point now has real customers awaiting its next release. Each project manager allocates monetary and people resources within an overall budget decided by the management team.

The global nature of Check Point meant that Triant and the Israeli management team had to agree on who was going to do what. The company is functionally divided with sales and marketing, business development, customer support, and public relations in the United States. Research and development and product strategy are based in Israel. Like the company, senior management is functionally divided. Schwed guides R&D in Israel, and Kramer, who has moved to the United States, handles operations. Triant is the public figure, communicating with Wall Street and the press, filling speaking engagements, and interacting with major customers. The demands of Check Point's bipolar culture have compelled Triant and her Israeli counterparts to put needed structure in place more swiftly than the norm at small companies, which could prove a decided advantage in the competitive arena of Internet security.

■ THE BOTTOM LINE

Any day now, some aspiring Jerry Seinfeld is going to walk into a television network's headquarters and pitch a story idea about life in a technology start-up. Indeed, Silicon Valley in particular and high tech in general have already been

VIEW FROM THE TOP

Tom Siebel, CEO, Siebel Systems

On Management:

"At Siebel Systems, we have a radical corporate culture and management philosophy. We've taken employee ownership to the max. We're 70 percent employee owned. When we think about customer and employee satisfaction, we don't think about nameless public shareholders, we think about the receptionist and the marketing administrator. We believe in alliances and have built the most virtual corporation in history."

On Being a Manager:

"I don't consider myself a manager. My skills are leadership skills. I've been very fortunate that there are very good managers who work here. I deal with strategic issues, set the vision. Whether it's designing a product, dealing with customer satisfaction, closing a deal, I manage by example. Between the meetings I am lowest on the tree. I am out executing—working with engineers, talking with customers, dealing with landlords. Management of the process is handled by other people."

On Innovation:

"We go out and talk to customers. Every idea we have, we go out to the customers. We don't get a lot of engineers in a room, lock them up and let them go crazy. We iterate with customers continually. When we deliver it, we know it's what they want. If one of our engineers has a breakthrough, we'll bring customers in and get feedback."

(continued)

VIEW FROM THE TOP (Continued)

On Moving into New Markets:

"We moved into a new area, customer service, last year. Our customers told us they wanted it. It wasn't like I went up a mountain and came down with a vision."

On Alliances:

"We've partnered where we don't have core competencies. We try to partner with the company that's the leader in their field. Instead of trying to do services ourselves, we went to Andersen, which has instant access to 45,000 professional service people and engages in large-scale systems deployment. For training we partnered with Cambridge Technology Partners. We're focused on delivering high-quality enterprise-class client-server software."

---

mythologized in novels like *The Bitch Goddess* (serialized in 1996 in *Upside* magazine), *Microserfs* (HarperCollins, 1996), and *The First $20 Million Is Always the Hardest* (Random House, 1997) as a place where people under extreme pressure scream at each other, get into fights in the parking lot, throw computers against the wall, and generally act like jerks. There is indisputably some of that kind of stuff going on. The pressure at a technology company to succeed is the fiercest I've seen in any industry. It is fed in part by negative emotions like egomania and greed—but also by more positive ones, like the desire to create lasting value and have what you do every day mean something to the world. The superficial trappings of high-tech culture do include colorful incidents and eccentric behavior, but underneath all that, any company that expects to cross the chasm to lasting success had better have a sturdy foundation grounded in a well-defined culture.

A widely held belief within the technology industry is that while big companies make the most money, small companies are more innovative, more flexible, and just more fun. In my swing through the companies described in this book, many people confided to me that they had joined or started entrepreneurial companies because that's where they're the happiest and where their jobs, indeed their lives, are the most fulfilling. Hence, the continual outpouring of talented programmers, marketers, and executives from large companies into small ones. Even well-managed large companies such as Hewlett-Packard and Sun Microsystems suffer from high turnover—their very success makes them the target of headhunters and venture capitalists who want to seed their new start-up with top-quality people.

Thanks to these eclectic influences, high-tech culture, even in a small company, is far from monolithic. It runs the gamut from HP conservatism to Israeli militarism, to trivia bowls, and margaritas on the patio. It can be centered around a personality, or diffused through a consensus model. The commonalities, though, include: tolerance of a very wide range of work and personal habits; treatment of everyone, from the CEO to the newest hire, as equals, with the ability to chide or question management without going through channels; profound aversion to any structure or bureaucracy that gets in the way of doing the job; and an overwhelming sense that "we're all in this together, and my contribution is as essential as anyone else's."

An identifiable, workable company culture is an essential element of high-tech success (though hardly the only one). It is one of the first constants that must be established. Before you undertake product development or marketing strategy or financial forecasting, you had better decide how you're going to treat people, because they're going to carry out everything else you want to do. "Companies need to be fairly self-conscious about the values and environments they want to create," maintains strategist Gary Hamel. This social dimension of business is often ignored by entrepreneurial companies—to their peril—in their rush to exploit new markets. The consequence: Most entrepreneurial companies eventually die. Says consultant Geoffrey Moore: "We're so obsessed with tornadoes—the early hypergrowth period—in high tech that we forget that Ford and General Motors are the two dominant auto makers based on what happened sixty or seventy years ago."

The companies described here are just starting to develop their social dimension and grapple with the issue of forming a stable culture without impeding innovation. In the next chapter, we'll look at a select set of larger, more mature but still entrepreneurial companies whose cultures have set the stage for greatness.

Chapter

4

Bigger Can Be Better: Maintaining Equilibrium

Just as smaller companies are eager to scale new heights by growing in market share and profitability, large, well-established companies strive to retain or expand their competitive position in the market. This is true of businesses in all industries, but the process takes on an interesting spin in high tech. As part of their strategy, established high-tech companies would like to retain the culture of smaller firms, but they find this is challenging to do, given the organizational and revenue demands of a big company, not to mention the space requirements. Small companies tend to be tucked away in a corner suite of one of the look-alike office buildings that sprout like weeds amid technology growth centers. This is in stark contrast to large companies, for whom space is a major concern. To get enough, they often build their own campuses (as these collections of edifices are generally titled). For instance, when I arrived at the sprawling campus of Cisco Systems in an industrial area of north San Jose, I walked across dozens of acres of parking lots. Fourteen years ago, Cisco didn't even exist; now the thousands of cars cramming the lots—and the skyline dotted with Cisco's gleaming buildings—are vivid reminders of the company's explosive growth.

Ultimately, success in the technology industry is related to size, or what's more accurately referred to as "critical mass." Small companies all lust after it—even as they trumpet their lean size and their flexibility. But companies selling into the corporate world must have critical mass to offer the breadth of products, expertise, and support that these customers want. That's one of the main reasons why Compaq Computer recently bought Digital Equipment, why IBM has been able to remain a business-to-business champion for so long. Increasingly, corporate MIS decisions are moving away from buying individualized, best-of-breed solutions—like the highest-ranked sales automation software—and toward an integrated solution in which all the pieces (or systems) fit together. Best-of-breed buying gives small companies with one or two innovative products more of a shot. But the demand for integrated solutions, to avoid the headaches and hassles of making disparate products work together, favors larger vendors like Microsoft and German software maker SAP AG. Critical mass is also vital in pushing the company's identity, product line, and brand name through distribution channels: computer stores, major retailers, discount chains, and so forth. These distributors devote most of their shelf space to larger vendors that offer a range of high-selling, dependable products and product suites.

Clearly, being "big" in the technology industry is a double-edged sword. Becoming a market leader is every start-up's dream, but entrepreneurial companies don't want to lose their ability to take risks, respond to the market in a heartbeat, and experiment with new products. And it is these attributes that large companies strive to retain as they push the boundaries of their product lines, services, and processes. No company, no matter how big, wants to be viewed as a monolith.

In this chapter we look at three very successful, although relatively young, "big" technology companies: PeopleSoft, in Pleasanton, California; 3Com, in Santa Clara; and Cisco. None of these companies has relinquished its small-company culture, and they all share three characteristics:

➤ They all grew up post–personal computer, but pre-Internet, and are now rushing to embrace the on-line world.

➤ They all sell into the corporate marketplace.

➤ They all can be considered outstanding by virtue of their achievements, their sterling reputations, their reach, and above all, their cultures.

■ PUTTING PEOPLE FIRST

With 1997 revenues at $805 million and a market capitalization of $7.5 billion, PeopleSoft is proof that nice companies led by nice guys can finish first, or at least a strong second! (Among enterprise application vendors, People-Soft overtook Oracle in 1997, coming in second to number one SAP.) CEO Dave Duffield, who began his career at notoriously bureaucratic IBM, eschews the trappings of the typical senior executive. At PeopleSoft, people answer their own phones, and there are no personal secretaries or executive parking lots. Duffield's office sports photos of his three young adopted children and several dogs, miniature schnauzers who sometimes accompany him to the office. The CEO is tall, lean, and obviously fit; only the shock of gray hair betrays his age—57—making him old enough to be a grandfather to PeopleSoft's youngest employees. When we met, Duffield asked that our meeting be completed by 4:15 P.M. so that he could attend his three-and-a-half-year-old daughter's final swim class. This paternal concern characterizes Duffield's approach to the workplace, while the core values and principles of the company stem from Duffield's own beliefs. *IndustryWeek* magazine made Duffield the subject of a February 1998 cover story, noting that "every ounce of PeopleSoft's corporate culture that both employees and customers experience can be traced to the pervasive influence of the founder." As this statement suggests, it is the corporate culture that has contributed to PeopleSoft's growth rate of 100 percent in 1997 by attracting new customers and retaining employees.

Duffield believes in being a nurturer, but he is quick to point out that this perspective in no way undermines the company's competitive instinct. "We hate to lose. We spend our energy selling our product in a high-intensity way. We're a bunch of nice guys kicking ass, but, internally, it's quite a love-in. People love working here," says Duffield. Love-fest, indeed! PeopleSoft's annual turnover rate is about 2 percent—phenomenal in an industry where 15 to 20 percent is the norm. In fact, PeopleSoft is so confident of its employees' loyalty that it permits head-hunters to solicit them openly via e-mail.

"We hate to lose. We spend our energy selling our product in a high-intensity way. We're a bunch of nice guys kicking ass, but, internally, it's quite a love-in."
—Dave Duffield, founder and CEO, PeopleSoft

"It sounds too good to be true." That's what Sarge Kennedy, an engineer who's now a research-and-development product manager for PeopleSoft, thought when he joined the company five years ago after a stint at Oracle. "Oracle's culture is very cutthroat, and that attitude was evident in how my managers treated me," he recalls. Kennedy found a home at PeopleSoft. "When I joined PeopleSoft, it had all the things that I loved and none that I hated. PeopleSoft combines an entrepreneur's passion with a professional management."

Almost a decade ago, PeopleSoft pioneered the development of human resources software. Although it still dominates this niche, the company recognized that the market is limited. With an eye toward greater expansion, People-Soft elected to move into the far more competitive arena known as enterprise resource planning (ERP). Besides human resources, ERP software handles manufacturing, distribution, and financials—all considered "mission-critical" to the major corporations that buy the expensive and complex products. Experts questioned whether People-Soft could go up against such formidable, already-entrenched rivals as SAP, which leads in the sector, or always-dangerous Oracle. PeopleSoft in 1995 was a $232 million company, small compared to its two competitors. "The company that Duffield built is tackling a lot of tough challenges at once," noted a November 1995 profile on PeopleSoft in *Upside* magazine. "Can PeopleSoft and its CEO disprove the notion that nice guys finish last?"

Three years later, the answer is a qualified "yes." PeopleSoft has successfully rolled out its new line of software, pushed revenues past $800 million annually, and served notice that you can be nice and decent and still take market share away from feisty Oracle and SAP. PeopleSoft has blossomed into a force to be reckoned with in the important market for ERP applications.

■ DAVE'S RULES OF BUSINESS BEHAVIOR

The corporate culture now entrenched at PeopleSoft is reinforced through the company's hiring practices; compensation systems; and office atmosphere, which supports self-actualization. PeopleSoft works hard to match the people it hires to its culture, and more than half of its new employees come from internal referrals. "We attract people who embrace our values. We have a market value of $7 billion and it's all in the people," says Duffield. "We would be foolish not to support an environment in which people like to excel." One way that PeopleSoft builds an environment of innovation and achievement is by setting up project teams that tackle one assignment, then break up so that their members can go on to something new. This approach helps to re-create the feeling of a start-up for each project. "You work on something and put your whole heart into it," says Kennedy. "After you master that, you have a new project you can work on. A new project is like a little family unto itself. I don't feel like it's a huge, faceless company even though there's 4,500 people."

"We attract people who embrace our values. We have a market value of $7 billion and it's all in the people."
—Dave Duffield, founder and CEO, PeopleSoft

Since joining PeopleSoft three years ago, Tina Cox, whose formal title is communications program manager, has become known as "the culture queen." That's in partnership with Duffield, who is "the culture god." Cox's primary job is that of establishing and maintaining internal communications with employees. She is aided by Heidi Kenniston, internal communications specialist, whose husband, Jeff, is a software developer at PeopleSoft. Cox and Kenniston have initiated programs that enhance the company's internal culture, introducing everything from "Taco Tuesdays" to five-year-service awards, and developing a formal statement on core values that voices the company's commitment to innovation, integrity, customers, quality, people, and fun. Kenniston, who worked for the government before coming to PeopleSoft, welcomed the reduction in bureaucracy. "I had to call Dave on the phone one day and he answered [it] himself. I thought I would get his voice mail, but I got him. That's when I knew that I can call on anyone here to help me do whatever I need to."

"A new project is like a little family unto itself. I don't feel like it's a huge, faceless company even though there's 4,500 people."
—Sarge Kennedy, engineer, PeopleSoft

Evidence of Duffield's management style and commitment to instilling a value system at PeopleSoft—and perhaps the highest expression of the company's culture—is a periodic memo that Duffield sends out entitled "Dave's Rules of Business Behavior" (see page 90). The memo covers such seemingly mundane items as cleaning water off the bathroom sink and putting your phone on do-not-disturb when you're away from your desk. "The memo is written the way Dave talks," says Cox. "I've seen a lot of people print this out and put it on their wall. Dave really believes that his role is fostering the culture." Kenniston still remembers the time she sent out a memo about a new program at PeopleSoft, and Duffield sent her a little note saying "good job" for this relatively routine matter. "Not every CEO would bother to take the time," she says.

Another example of the trust that exists at PeopleSoft is that, unlike many technology companies which have firm rules against recruiting on campus, PeopleSoft doesn't bother to enforce any restrictions. "Other organizations come after our people all the time," says Cox. "If you want to be recruited, you are recruitable. We don't put any huge walls up. Employees openly talk on our internal database about recruiters, but no one wants to go anywhere else." Part of the reason for this remarkable level of employee retention is that PeopleSoft is very open with all its employees, both in terms of their own performance and with company-wide situations. For instance, when PeopleSoft's usually high-flying share price was getting hammered in a market downturn (and employees all have stock options), chief financial officer Rod Codd posted an e-mail explaining why the stock price was so rocky.

With revenues clearly skyrocketing and employee and customer satisfaction at an all-time high, it all adds up to what sounds like a corporate Eden. If there's a snake in that Eden, it's what happens to the company when Duffield eventually leaves. Although he is not planning on leaving in the near future, succession planning can never start too early, expecially when so much of the company's success derives from its leader. As one executive at Dun & Bradstreet pointed out, "In many ways, PeopleSoft and Dave Duffield are one and the same. What is PeopleSoft without Dave Duffield?"

Author/consultant Gary Hamel cites two characteristics of a company that is destined for lasting greatness:

1. Being able to remake itself after its original idea fades.
2. Outliving the first generation of leadership, thus demonstrating that there's more there than a single driving personality.

PeopleSoft has successfully expanded its product and market base from human resources to ERP; now it is crucial to ensure that the culture that underlies so much of the company's prosperity will be sustained by the next generation of management. Says Duffield: "Part of my job and the management team's job is to pick a potential successor who embodies the same kind of values and spirit that I do." Plenty of people, he adds, "could do a better job in driving revenues and profits or products, but to provide the culture leadership is much more difficult." PeopleSoft is a living example of how a low-key, genial CEO can lead by example and maintain a lasting familial culture even in the face of tremendous growth.

■ THE NEXT GENERATION

The two companies profiled in the next few sections have both survived and flourished under a second or third generation of leadership. In fact, one of them, 3Com Corporation, might not have survived if there hadn't been a change at the top. The other company, Cisco, is on its third CEO and has flourished under each of them. Although they each began in different spheres, 3Com and

Cisco, based in the adjoining cities of Santa Clara and San Jose, California, are now competing in one of the hottest areas of technology: networking. Both Cisco and 3Com have become multibillion-dollar enterprises thanks to the huge, virtually insatiable need for their products among corporations.

■ SURVIVING CHANGES IN LEADERSHIP, AGAIN AND AGAIN

3Com was founded in 1979, but in a way it's younger than Cisco, which was founded in 1984, because 3Com redefined its position in the marketplace and its corporate mission under its second CEO. 3Com's reincarnation began in 1990 under Eric Benhamou, who joined the company as CEO as the result of a merger with Bridge Communications. (See Chapter 10 for a fuller description of 3Com's turnaround.) The Algerian-born, French-educated Benhamou seldom raises his voice. He doesn't have to. So great is the respect he commands within 3Com that the slightest hint of his displeasure, like quietly dropping his hand upon a table, is enough to get the attention of everyone in the room.

> "I think confrontation of people in general is more negative than positive."
>
> —Eric Benhamou, CEO, 3Com

Compactly built, with dark, gray-tinged hair and a black mustache, Benhamou is an engineer by training and at heart. He solves problems, whether involving technology or people, in an analytical rather than emotional manner, without accusing but also without backing down. "I confront issues but rarely people," he says. "I think confrontation of people in general is more negative than positive. Many people on the receiving end don't make the distinction between attacking the issues and attacking them. Confrontation works fine for a group of people who have self-confidence and are fairly homogeneous. But as a company gets bigger and more diversified and you're in with a group of people you've never worked with before, it can be devastating."

Barbara Shapiro, vice president of corporate communications and a 3Com employee since 1986, calls Benhamou a "quiet aggressor. He doesn't rant or rave, but it's clear by his demeanor that he means business." Benhamou, she says, "leads by vision. He's a clear thinker and very articulate. He trusts the people who work for him. The expectation is that you're a leader in your own right and will apply your expertise to your job." Notes Debra Engel, senior vice president of corporate services: "It's very rare that you see any emotion from Eric. I can count on the fingers of one hand the times I've thought he was angry. When he does get angry, it's when someone is not being a team player and continuing an argument past the point of discussion, wasting time. For Eric, it's time to join up and move on."

➤ Meritocracy Personified

3Com's culture and corporate vision is reflective of Benhamou's own personal drive and priorities. Born into a Jewish family on the border between Algeria and Morocco, Benhamou and his family fled to France during the Algerian war in 1960. Later, Benhamou emigrated to the United States with his parents, ultimately earning a master's degree from Stanford University. After experiencing prejudice both as a refugee and a Jew, Benhamou is firmly dedicated to the principles of meritocracy and diversity at 3Com. Explains Engel: "There are no entitlements here. Your power and your rewards are a function of the value you add to the company. Hierarchy is not a determining factor." 3Com prides itself on being a company of knowledgeable workers "who have to engage their heads, their hearts, and their passion." At 3Com, bonuses and stock options are based on performance—employees can earn up to half their base pay in bonuses and several times their pay in equity.

The ideals of meritocracy are reinforced through 3Com's organizational policies. For example, employees don't report time on the job. It's assumed that they can monitor themselves and be responsible. Another example is in 3Com's travel policy, where any employee, regardless of title or level, who travels over so many thousands of miles is eligible for first-class travel. After debating whether to limit access to information or impose limitations on stock trading, 3Com chose the latter. "We believe that our employees, as partners, should have access to all information," says Engel, but the tradeoff is that all employees must abide by restrictions on when they can trade their stock. From human resources policies regarding travel to the rules that impact the financial core of the company, 3Com is rigorous in ensuring that every program and even the physical workplace itself reinforce the organization's devotion to a democratic work environment.

At the core of Benhamou's management style is his commitment to distributed leadership and decision-making. His analytical nature differs from Duffield's nurturing approach but is just as effective. For Benhamou, there is no limit on what can be achieved—and for this reason he is extremely demanding of his management team and of himself. Benhamou is a firm believer in teamwork, and he promotes bonding through Outward Bound–type outings where executives are challenged to walk across a desert or leap off a cliff into a pool of water. Members of his management team have crossed a desert in Israel, symbolizing 3Com's virtual return from the dead. They have climbed a mountain in the Sierras and hiked down a steep, narrow trail in Arizona. At the end of that trail was a 50-foot vertical drop where executives had to make a choice: Rappel down the cliff or leap into a pool of water that was only a little bigger than the table in 3Com's conference room. Most of the team, including Benhamou, jumped.

Engel, who has been on every one of these trips, says that they bind the management team closer together by creating shared adventures. The trip she got the most out of was crossing the Israeli desert and then bobbing around in the Dead Sea. "For Eric, it was a way of sharing something of himself, which he doesn't typically do. There was a real feeling of family." There is no penalty for saying no to the various challenges on these trips, though the presence of your CEO participating in every event right beside you is a big incentive to push your own limits. "This is not a college frat house," says Engel. "They don't goad or harass anyone. We push ourselves and try to support each other. When you hit your limit, that's okay too." The trips are not done in isolation, but in conjunction with meetings where everyone talks about the company's performance and how things can be done better.

Benhamou points out that to truly operate as a team, managers have to get to know each other in different settings. "If we go climb a mountain together or go canyoneering, it's different than having a dinner. There's an atmosphere of intensity and risk-taking that requires the team to come together. It's also more thrilling."

Like his outdoor adventures, Benhamou brings the thrills back home. It was he who engineered the largest acquisition in 3Com's history and one of the largest in the technology industry: an $8.5 billion takeover of U.S. Robotics Corporation. The same kind of risk-taking led him to reposition 3Com from a hardware company into a software innovator in 1990. "Being able to feel comfortable about risk is very important in this industry. I find it normal to take all kinds of risks," Benhamou says. That's why he considers his company a meritocracy: You take risks to get to the top. There's no room for playing it safe and covering your ass here. With this kind of leadership and the go-for-broke culture it has engendered, 3Com may stumble again—but it will certainly pick itself up and go on.

"Being able to feel comfortable about risk is very important in this industry."

—Eric Benhamou, CEO, 3Com

■ SERENDIPITY BABY! ON A HIGH HORSE WITH CISCO

Cisco is one of those companies that happens to find itself
in the right place at the right time. In 1984, Leonard Bo-
sack and Sandy Lerner, then husband and wife attending
Stanford University, devised a way to connect computer
networks by utilizing an electronic router. (Acting, in effect, like an electronic postal service, a router breaks information up into small pieces, or packets, and directs
them to their destination via the Internet or some other
network.) The couple founded Cisco, selling routers almost casually by means of the Internet and word of mouth
for several years.

With the proliferation of computer networks, business
boomed, and soon Cisco was bursting through revenue
milestones. After the start-up evolved into an established
business, requiring a more formalized structure and a sophisticated management team, its founders were ready to
relinquish their positions to a successor. Lerner (whose
most recent claim to fame was posing nude atop a horse in
the July 7, 1997 issue of *Forbes* magazine) and her husband
departed the company in 1990, shortly after it went public,
reaping almost $200 million from their Cisco stock.

John Morgridge, a technology industry veteran, joined
Cisco in 1988 as president and CEO, positions he held until
January 1995, when he turned the reins over to Cisco's
current CEO, John Chambers. Morgridge remains as the
chairman and public spokesman for the company. As CEO
and now as chairman, Morgridge can be credited with
shaping Cisco's culture, which evolved as the company
grew into a $6.4 billion behemoth with more than 11,000

employees. Today, Cisco has joined the ranks of such high-tech titans as Microsoft and Intel, as a dominant player in a critical technology arena.

Morgridge and Chambers make an interesting contrast. Morgridge, who is 64, is laid-back, candid, and dryly humorous; everyone in the company has a favorite Morgridge witticism. Chambers is 48, high-energy, and relentlessly cheerful. Cisco has prospered under three very different regimes by running lean and mean from a financial perspective, while encouraging a large amount of individualism in its product-development ranks, made up of engineers and entrepreneurs drawn from dozens of acquired companies.

Cisco generates nearly $600,000 in annual revenue per employee, which is even better than Microsoft. Cisco's frugality is legendary. One example is that all employees, including Morgridge himself, fly coach unless they use frequent-flyer miles to upgrade. "The company pays for coach," says Morgridge. Although he owns nearly 10 million Cisco shares (worth $850 million in late 1997), Morgridge confides that he takes advantage of senior-citizen discount coupons, available to people over 62, to upgrade. "We've never been against best value," he says. "It's not how much you spend, but how much value you get." Barbara Beck, Cisco's vice president of human resources, has an addendum. She still laughs when recalling Morgridge's presentation on frugality at a directors' meeting. He set up chairs onstage in the configuration of coach versus business class and suggested that instead of moaning about coach, people could go *virtually* first class by "picking up the mask and slippers on your way through the first-class cabin."

Morgridge ran Cisco in the late 1980s and early 1990s with a management team of eight people, but subsequent growth, he says, has dictated a new structure. Now there is a layer of senior vice presidents, and numerous vice presidents, many of whom are the former heads of companies that Cisco bought. (Cisco has acquired 25 companies since 1993.) Although Chambers is a more professional-type manager, Morgridge says the two of them are similar in that they "always challenge people." Morgridge recalls hiring a "company shrink" to assess Cisco's diverse culture, who told him, "This is the only company I've ever been in where you can say to anyone, 'No, you're wrong.' " This tolerance for individualism verging on chaos is important—innovation cannot occur in a company where deviation is suspect. You have to give people room to make mistakes in order for them to make leaps forward.

In some ways, Cisco has matured to reflect the more traditional corporate model. Structure has become more formal at the top, as the handoff from Morgridge to Chambers demonstrates. Chambers had been with the company for four years as an executive vice president when he was elevated to the top position. Says Morgridge: "He was hired with the understanding that if he performed, he was the heir apparent. When he actually became CEO, it was not a surprise. It was a planned succession. If you don't do that you can have a lot of internal competition that's unhealthy." He adds, with typical Morgridge irony, "The mistake in our industry is not that chief executives leave too early; it's that they stay too long." Morgridge wanted to pilot Cisco over the billion-dollar mark in revenues before moving on. He achieved this milestone in fiscal year 1994. "It is clear that this could be a $10 billion company. I felt it was important that we had someone like John who had that as a goal. There was no way I was going to be here that long," he says.

"The mistake in our industry is not that chief executives leave too early; it's that they stay too long."
—John Morgridge, Chairman, Cisco Systems

➤ Sealed with a Handshake

In many other ways, however, Cisco has retained the informality of a small company. Krish Ramakrishnan came on board in 1995 after Cisco bought the company he founded,

Internet Junction. The deal occurred with a handshake after lunch with Chambers. The discussion "was not like what you imagine when you're trying to sell a company," says Ramakrishnan. "It was more like I was interviewing for a job rather than selling my company. John put me at ease. What he was trying to figure out was whether we would be successful in Cisco's environment. John's opinion is that if the people fit, everything else will work out." When the time came to assimilate Ramakrishnan's small start-up, Cisco decided the best way to do that was to locate his group within the executive staff. So a 10-person engineering team worked on the same floor with Chambers and other executives. That way, the new group could get to know Cisco's leadership. It was a way to reproduce the feeling of being in a start-up, where everyone works side by side.

"Within six months of the acquisition, we had a product ready for the Cisco router," Ramakrishnan recalls. He and his team have now moved to a different location as part of a larger business unit, making way for later acquisitions to repeat their experience. "Cisco pays attention to the people behind the product. The people get integrated first," he says. Ramakrishnan admires Cisco's ability to bring entrepreneurial teams on board without overpowering them with structure. Both Morgridge and Chambers are committed to decentralized management and empowering people.

➤ A Solid Core with Fuzzy Edges

Morgridge isn't convinced that a single, well-defined culture is necessarily good for a company. "Some of the early mainframe computer companies had strongly defined cultures—and look what happened to them." Cisco integrated a number of cultures, yet at its core are a handful of underlying values that have always applied: frugality, opportunity, and humility. "The founders, particularly Sandy Lerner, contributed a couple of qualities: listening to the customer, staying close to the market," Morgridge notes. "We haven't deviated from those."

Beck identifies the company's core cultural values as commitment to the customer; fiscal conservatism; and concentration on results, not processes. "We're not a company that's procedure-driven," she says. "This is one of the most trusting organizations around. When we do expense reports for trips, managers get an e-mail notification and they authorize it electronically, usually without even seeing it." What's changed with growth is that the values are now consciously articulated. In the early years, frugality was a necessity because entrepreneurial Cisco had to conserve its cash. "Now we do it as a concerted effort to do more with less. That doesn't mean we always do it the cheapest way," she says. Indeed, the company is a generous patron to the local educational system, a tradition started by Morgridge. When Cisco was located in Menlo Park, "John walked across the street to the school district and said 'Let's establish a partnership,'" Beck recalls. Cisco wound up partnering with a nearby school that was strapped for funds, donating money and labor to blacktop and re-landscape the grounds. The company also provided a full-time employee to educate teachers about technology.

What Cisco has is "a solid core and fuzzy edges," as Beck puts it. Individual projects are handled by small teams which interact with customers and have considerable decision-making authority. A fast-start task force, with representatives from all levels of the company, evaluates productivity and offers suggestions for improvement. For example, any one of the hundreds of new employees that Cisco is bringing on can click on a "fast-start" button on the company Web page, which provides a shortcut to benefits information, the organizational chart, and other internal information. They can also enroll in a two-day training program offered via the Web. Within the first six months, says Beck, "we expect people, whether they're administrative, engineering or whatever, to understand the industry, products, and the end-to-end solution we offer, and how they fit in. We teach employees to write their own objectives and review them with their manager, rather than have the manager do it."

Cisco's biggest hurdle, ironically, may be its unprecedented rise. It has never really had a serious setback. 3Com's Benhamou believes his company is stronger for having gone through a retrenchment, while Cisco, he warns, is in danger of being "spoiled by success." Retorts Morgridge: "This company has always been very self-critical. We've never believed we were the smartest or had all the answers. We made enough mistakes." One he cites was failing to buy a competitive company, Vitalink, in the early 1990s. "We thought we didn't have to buy them; we could just hire all their salespeople and engineers." He admits this was one time when Cisco was too frugal. "Buying Vitalink would have accelerated our growth." Morgridge doesn't think Cisco will have too many swelled heads. Now that it's so big, "We have a lot of help in figuring out our mistakes because the press tells us all about them."

Of the three companies in this chapter, Cisco is the hardest to define. It is a kaleidoscope of tiny bits of culture from this company and that one, even while it projects a cool efficiency to the customers it serves. It was personality-driven in its early incarnation, but has deliberately moved toward decentralization and empowerment under Morgridge and Chambers. It has veteran executives at the top, but manages to provide continuing challenges to dozens of young, hungry, eager entrepreneurs, like Ramakrishnan, who could leave whenever they want to. In short, Cisco is something that works when you wouldn't expect it to; the solidity of its core is enhanced by the chaos at its outer bounds.

■ THE BOTTOM LINE

Marketing guru Regis McKenna says, "You can't act like a small company when you're a big company. When you're a big company, you have to get structured." But structure is

VIEW FROM THE TOP

John Morgridge, Chairman and former CEO, Cisco Systems

On Innovation:

"I define innovation broadly. Cisco innovated across the total spectrum, [for example] our unique leasing arrangement for land and buildings, our whole use of the Internet, our stock options, our manufacturing strategy."

On Winning Mind Share:

"We have the mind share of people who buy our kind of equipment. When we go into the home we have a challenge. We've got to come up with some innovative way to reach them."

On Growth at Cisco:

"It started with the market. The first thing we did correctly was find the market and focus on it. Whatever the customer wanted we'd respond to. We were not caught up in some particular religious feeling about any protocol. We've been very lucky. We were in the sweet spot."

On Succession Planning:

"The mistake in our industry is not that chief executives leave too early; it's that they stay too long. I had mentally committed to making the company a billion-dollar company before I stepped down. We reached that in fiscal '94, which ended in July 1994. It was clear this company could be a $10 billion company. I felt it was important that we had someone running it who had that as a goal. There was no way I was going to be here that long. They say this is a young man's game; there is the sheer physical factor of it.

(continued)

VIEW FROM THE TOP (Continued)

Long hours, online all the time, electronically bound to the machine 24 by 7."

On the Role of Chairman:

"There's the figurehead chairman who attends board meetings and isn't on-site at all. There's the chairman who just has a personal relationship with the president/CEO. And, there's the chairman who is the public persona for the company, and this is my role at Cisco. I speak to things that I have an interest in, like education, networking for schools. My second focus is government. I represent the company in Washington on issues like NAFTA and securities litigation. I have to be willing to invest the time to stay in touch."

---

not viewed fondly within technology companies. Remember Check Point, which established a structure by default, only when it couldn't be avoided. Geoffrey Moore says that companies that have emerged from their growth spurt (which he calls the tornado) with a hypercompetitive management style intact "may have no place to turn that energy. They could end up destroying or alienating each other." This is often the time when the company recruits a more seasoned executive team that can install a little structure and stability. "If you're going to stick with the hypergrowth competitive management," says Moore, "you have to keep finding a new tornado"—like Intel has with each succeeding generation of chips.

However, most big companies wind up with stable, revenue-producing products that to their creators lack some of the thrill generated by a brand-new market entry—a situation that Moore refers to as Main Street. "When I was talking to a group at Microsoft about Mi-

DAVE'S RULES

This is a slightly edited version of the memo on "Dave's Rules of Business Behavior" that PeopleSoft CEO Dave Duffield has sent out to his employees several times. This version was sent in June 1997.

To: PS-Staff
Subject: Dave's Rules of Business Behavior

I sent out this note approximately one year ago, when PeopleSoft had about half the people we do today. Consequently, it is twice as applicable today.

I've been thinking over the past few weeks and months that we have a pretty good thing going here at PeopleSoft. We're sort of like a family in many ways. As most of us remember from our youth, Mom and Dad had certain rules for the family to operate as cohesively as possible, and with great respect for each other. So it is, here at the PeopleSoft family.

Since some consider me the Father of PeopleSoft, I've come up with my personal set of Business Rules that I feel each of us should follow so that we can all live as harmoniously as possible. These are not the onerous policies you'd expect to find at Oracle or SAP—just simple steps we should be taking day-by-day to make life truly great for all that work at and visit PeopleSoft. These are by no means complete, and I expect to update them from time to time.

But to get started, here goes:

Business Rule #1. Keep the Restrooms Clean.

Yes, I've been associated with this Business Rule from the early days of PeopleSoft, and it's even more important now than it was then. I remember either listening to, or reading from, one of Tom Peters' famous books on Customer Ser-

(continued)

DAVE'S RULES (Continued)

vice. He gave an example of a passenger getting onto a plane, sitting down, and finding his fold-down tray covered with some mung from the previous flight—probably left by some Oracle sales guy who's still can't quite master the knife and fork. The passenger's thought: "Wow. If they can't handle the easy things like keeping the aircraft clean, how can they possibly deal with the hard things like engine maintenance?"

The customer/prospect analogy at PeopleSoft: "Wow, if they can't keep the restrooms clean, how can they possibly develop quality software products?"

So, please pay attention to the little things like keeping the restrooms, kitchens, hallways, and other public places—even your personal work area—as clean as possible. Our prospects and customers will think more kindly toward our products and services.

Business Rule #2. When Away, Use DND.
(DND = Do Not Disturb)

Most everyone is guilty of not using DND, and most everyone has been frustrated when trying to phone a fellow employee and have the phone ring five times, only to find the person is away from his/her desk. This is equally frustrating to customers and prospects trying to reach us. They probably think, "If they don't have the courtesy of placing their phones on DND, I can't imagine what their restrooms look like."

So, when you're away from your desk for more than 10 seconds, place your phone on DND. In this manner, any person trying to reach you will immediately receive your voice message, and will not have to wait for the five rings to finish. Equally important, your adjacent coworkers can remain productive rather than being steamed at you for leaving your phone on YDD (Yes, Do Disturb). And keep in

(continued)

DAVE'S RULES (Continued)

mind, there are a bunch of crazies out there who would think nothing of blowing away their own family members for lesser crimes than not using DND.

Business Rule #3. Keep Up with Your Voicemail.

How many of us enjoy the all-too-familiar "Phonemail system voice storage is full. Please delete those messages which are not needed."? And there's no way to bypass this sucker. A career side-benefit: If you keep up with your voicemail, people will actually think you're doing work, even though you're probably out on the golf course.

Business Rule #4. Don't Kiss Up and Slap Down.

This is mostly a rule for people who have other people working for them (or, at least think they do). We've had—I emphasize HAD—a couple of people at PeopleSoft who thought proper business behavior was to play business kissy-face with one's boss, and possibly the boss's boss, all the while playing slappy-face with the people they manage. In other words, they play Jacqueline Kennedy Onassis with their superiors and Attila the Hun with those they manage.

It's a good career idea at PeopleSoft to behave consistently regardless of who you're dealing with. Treat fellow employees, customers, prospects, suppliers, and the bagel delivery people with the same respect and courtesy you'd offer the late Jerry Garcia.

Business Rule #5. Don't Attach Big-Mother Files to Your Notes.

How many of us have been out on some Caribbean island, one or more rum concoctions in hand, attached to the local phone system (where the rates are published in bold,

(continued)

DAVE'S RULES (Continued)

24-point sans serif type), replicating your mail file, only to wait an eternity to get that one important message—something about an HR demonstration to a Florida-based men's lingerie company for the vertically challenged? You might have to go through another rum thing or two before the replication is complete. Frustrating, isn't it?

Business Rule #6. Paging and Productivity Are Antonyms.

How many times have you been involved with desk-checking a four-dimensional loop of actuarial calculations when from overhead you hear: "Anthony Damaschino, please dial *81, Anthony Damaschino, *81."? It's back to the beginning of desk-checking for you. Not only is this antiproductive for you, your coworkers, and our receptionist, but Anthony doesn't like to have his name mentioned in public.

So, please use the paging capabilities only when absolutely necessary. In fact, I've asked several antipaging enthusiasts to craft their own business rule for paging. Here goes:

"Excessive paging and unmonitored ringing telephones are disruptive to coworkers. Realistically determining your availability and communicating this to your customers and coworkers will allow for fewer interruptions and greater accessibility to everyone."

There you have it—the first cut at Dave's Rules of Business Behavior. As other suggestions are made, I'll be sure to consider them for future releases. Since we're still growing at our 100 percent annual rate, and since so many new people join PeopleSoft each month, I plan on sending this note to everyone on a more frequent basis.

Thanks again for being here, and I expect you're still having fun.

crosoft Office, one of the engineers said the booby prize is we're on Main Street and it's not interesting anymore," Moore recounts. "That's the engineer mentality—'If I'm not on the cutting edge I'm not interested.' " But part of innovation is to create products that appeal to a broad user base; not fabulous breakthroughs but dependable platforms upon which other members of the value chain can build. "That's why," he notes, "a whole lot of engineers cash out and go back to the beginning of the game [i.e., a start-up]. It's like people who ride the *Star Wars* ride at Disney-land again and again."

Large organizations must have a functional structure: (i.e., accounting, human resources, sales, and the like). "You start looking like the classic organizational charts," Moore says, "but those very disciplines which are key to not making mistakes also stifle innovation." What counters that is small teams that cut across functional lines and allow innovation to flourish in an intrapreneurial fashion. What I observed time and again was that successful big companies, like the three cited here, treat these product teams like a portfolio of investments. They assess the team projects in the way a venture capitalist or mutual fund manager would, and shift their funds from one to another depending on the promise. This model enables a large company to maintain the entrepreneurial atmosphere so essential to growth. As we've said, to stand still in this fast-moving industry is to confine yourself to the equivalent of a biological dead end: a species that is no longer evolving and which will ultimately disappear.

Having small, empowered teams is merely the first step to survival. What must reinforce that is what People-Soft, 3Com, and Cisco have: a foundation of core values that bind you together, yet allow for flexibility and adaptation. Small or large, what companies must have is a tolerance for chaos, or as Cisco puts it, "fuzzy edges." Technology companies have learned that it's no longer possible to rigidly order the world in which you compete, and your internal structure must reflect that reality. PeopleSoft has split off more and more internal teams to keep chaos within. Cisco and 3Com have done it that way as well as through numerous acquisitions. GeoPartners' consultant Jim Moore likens the use of multiple teams to what's known as "parallel processing" in computers. Rather than having one massive super machine, parallel processing links together a series of microprocessors within smaller computers, enhancing flexibility and allowing many problems to be solved simultaneously.

"With the best companies, the excitement level is just as high at large companies as at start-ups. You have to figure out how to keep the excitement up and not let infrastructure get in the way."

—Joe K. Carter, Andersen Consulting

Chapter

Staking Your Claim: Finding and Keeping New Markets

Earlier in this book I described how the high-tech industry can be compared to the nineteenth-century California Gold Rush, as aspiring entrepreneurs rush to stake their claim to new markets. In fact, being first to recognize and exploit a new market is the chief advantage of small companies. Many technology start-ups are created to serve a niche that's below the radar screen of larger companies with established customer bases. IBM, for example, was so dedicated to its lucrative mainframe business that it missed out on the PC market that it might have claimed for its own. Similarly, Apple could have held on to the PC market had it been willing to open up its design and allow clones of the hugely successful Macintosh. Instead, it remained committed to a proprietary strategy. Now the companies making Wintel clones have taken over the market. And we don't even need to talk about Microsoft missing the Internet, although it has recovered admirably!

Because technology developments occur so rapidly, particularly in the Internet arena, high-tech start-ups operate like the gold-rush miner, staking claims based on guesswork or instinct or hope. Robert Reid, venture capitalist and author of *Architects of the Web,* accurately applies the gold-rush metaphor: "You have to stake your claim before you can start mining it, not knowing if the business model is going to pan out." As an example, he notes two Internet pioneers, Netscape Communications and Yahoo!, which gave away their first products, respectively a browser and a Net directory service, in order to stake their claim. "They were looking to own their space and didn't even think about a revenue model until later," says Reid.

"You have to stake your claim before you can start mining it, not knowing if the business model is going to pan out."
—Robert Reid, author of *Architects of the Web* and venture capitalist, 21st Century Internet Venture Partners

---

Venture capitalists are more eager to invest in a company that they think can own a brand-new market than in one that offers an improved version of an already-existing product. "We're looking for people willing to think big, who want to take over the world," says renowned venture capitalist Ann Winblad. "It's easier to scale back than to scale up." The first company that starts supplying a new market can publicize itself as the market leader. Generally, new and growing markets can support at least two major competitors, so the second company in is also successful. This is why PeopleSoft was able to capture significant market share in the ERP market, even though SAP was the established leader. The entrance of a strong competitor helps to validate the market and assuage federal antitrust investigators. But be third or fourth, and, unless you're a Microsoft or Oracle, with lots of capital and muscle to put behind your effort, you'll be scratching to survive.

Analyst and investor Howard Anderson of the Yankee Group sums it up, "If you're a start-up, you figure out a new market that a fat old company missed and get there earlier. While the mature company considers how to enter the new market without cannibalizing its existing base, the small company keeps innovating, and by the time the big guy catches up they've got 37 percent of the market." With the technology industry itself getting older, the number of experienced people leaving companies to join start-ups is growing by leaps and bounds. No niche goes undetected for long. "There's a herd mentality," says Anderson. "You'll suddenly find eight companies in a $10 million market. Look at palmtop computing—the market was never there, but there were 10 or 11 start-ups." With his customary practicality, Anderson offers two rules for identifying an overplayed niche: "If there's an industry association, it's too late. And, if there's a major trade show, it's too late."

The two routes for entering a new market are these: (1) Create or fully exploit a paradigm shift; and (2) identify a niche that is not being served well and become the market leader in that niche.

Companies that effectively used the first strategy—taking advantage of a paradigm shift—are Microsoft, Apple, Netscape, and Yahoo!, the first two of whom made the move from mainframe to personal computers and the latter two from stand-alone PCs to the Internet. Each was originally a start-up in a new-product arena that could have easily been dominated by a more established player (IBM in the case of Microsoft and Apple; Microsoft in the case of Netscape and Yahoo!), but the larger companies did not recognize these new market needs as a viable part of their business.

The second strategy—defining a niche that is not being served and enter that arena—is sometimes the only one available, since you can't always guarantee a paradigm shift. We saw this strategy work at Cisco Systems and at CrossWorlds Software. "The single most important thing a high-tech company can do is to pick the right segment," sums up Anderson. "If you pick the right segment and don't execute perfectly, you'll [still] be okay. If you pick the wrong segment, you're doomed no matter how well the strategy is executed."

■ CREATING A MARKET: SURFING FOR INTERNET REVENUES

Yahoo! is definitely one company that picked the right segment. Located in Santa Clara, Yahoo! began life as an Internet search company and evolved into a new-media company. Yahoo! has grown into a global network of branded sites offering Web navigation as well as aggregated content, merchant services, and communication services. In June 1998, it was used by an audience of over 40 million people worldwide. When you enter Yahoo!'s headquarters, you know you're in a nontraditional company. The lobby is decked out in Yahoo!'s corporate colors: vivid shapes of purple and yellow. Meeting with executives there, I waited on a purple couch that looked like a refugee from a frat house and stared at a large neon sign on the yellow wall opposite me that asked: "Do You Yahoo!?" The typical cubicles are decorated with gold paper stars bearing the name of the occupant and the ubiquitous "Do You Yahoo!?" Conference rooms are named after the 10 biblical plagues of ancient Egypt; the one reserved for my meeting was titled "Pestilence."

But for all its "in-your-face" attitude (or maybe because of it) Yahoo! is one of a handful of companies that are actually making money from the Internet. San Francisco investment bank Hambrecht & Quist projected that Yahoo!, which is profitable, would have over $165 million in revenue in fiscal 1998—only three years after its formal founding and two years after it went public. Its market cap in early 1998 was $3 billion—the same as companies fifty times its size in revenues, like Silicon Graphics or

Apple. Yahoo! has made a lot of people rich, including its young founders, David Filo and Jerry Yang, who in 1997 endowed a $2 million chair at their alma mater, Stanford University. As in the days of early railroad baron Leland Stanford, there's no mistaking the influence of high-tech wealth. Stanford's board of trustees approved the name "Yahoo! Founders Professor" for the new chair, the first time an exclamation point (which Yahoo! insists is part of its company name) has ever been part of a Stanford professor's title.

Filo and Yang were young doctoral students at Stanford when they started the whimsically named Yahoo! (after those ignorant creatures in *Gulliver's Travels*) as a hobby in April 1994. Housed in a trailer, the Internet directory service was launched to help fellow students navigate the new medium. Its use spread by word of mouth. "Jerry and I did this for a year at Stanford," says Filo, whose business card still bears the title *Chief Yahoo*. "We never thought about making money from it. It was more about keeping the service going and having fun." But because it was providing a much-needed function—a way to find what you wanted on the newly emerging Internet—Yahoo! grew so fast that Filo and Yang dropped their doctoral studies and recruited some of their fellow students to work with them.

In April 1995, the two presented their nascent Internet company to Sequoia Capital of Menlo Park and came away with $1 million in seed funding. Michael Moritz, a general partner in the venture capital firm, recalls that Yahoo! already had competition in the form of other search engine companies which had almost simultaneously jumped into the market. (No potential gold mine goes uncharted for long.) "We wrote the check because we saw that the company had no deadwood, just two characters who wanted to go as quickly as they possibly could," Moritz recalls. "They had no agendas or constituencies. All the other companies had more people, competing tensions, and prejudices. We were able to get Yahoo! going quickly because as soon as we talked to them we had a collective idea on how we wanted to proceed."

Yahoo!'s founders were willing to do whatever was necessary to be the first to stake a claim to this new market. That meant turning over control of their company to a seasoned chief executive and management team. Filo recalls, "I didn't aspire to be Bill Gates. Jerry and I were interested in starting a company and seeing where we could take it. We didn't have the time to learn how to do this stuff, so it was in our best interest to bring in people who had grown a company before." Filo and Yang's approach reflects an interesting combination of a number of strategies already covered in this book: They relinquished the CEO position to a seasoned professional as preparation to grow the company; and they recognized a paradigm shift and threw themselves into it, becoming the market leader with the support of a venture capitalist backer.

"We didn't have the time to learn how to do this stuff, so it was in our best interest to bring in people who had grown a company before."

—David Filo, founder, Yahoo!

Enter Tim Koogle, brought in as CEO by the founders to fully exploit the new claim. Prior to joining Yahoo!, Koogle, who is 46 years old, had 15 years of executive management experience in high tech, as well as stints at Motorola and Seattle-based Intermec. Like Yang and Filo, he had an engineering degree from Stanford, and even though he was president of a company in Seattle, he still kept a home in the Bay Area. Despite the nearly 20-year difference in their ages, Koogle and the two founders discovered they had a lot in common. With longish graying hair and world-weary good looks, Koogle resembles a former hippie. He peppers his conversation with references to Zen and other esoteric subjects. And he definitely hit it off with Yang and Filo.

After joining the company in mid-1995, Koogle concentrated on devising a formal business plan. He and the founders wrote a 20-page document outlining the company's strategy for building a large, profitable enterprise. The plan stipulated that Yahoo! would deliver the best navigational guide functionality on the Web. "We've always been clear about that," says Koogle. "It's at the center of what we do." The business plan also suggested that if Yahoo! was successful at providing comprehensive navigation of the Web, it could attract millions of users who would show by their consumption exactly what they found popular in the new medium. The company then would partner with content providers, merchants, and communication services providers to bring users what they want, in essence vertically integrating through partnerships.

Today, Yahoo! has evolved to become a "media" company providing content around its navigational guide, including weather, news and financial information, classified job and personal listings, a Web guide for kids, an interactive site for women, and regional and international guides. Yahoo! has become akin to a television network on the Web, collecting content produced by independent studios. "We're not in the original content creation business," says Koogle. "We do what all well-run network businesses do: Aggregate content which is authored by independent sources, then 'program' it, brand it, and distribute it. The business model we established is very similar to that of a broadcast network. We offer the use of the content for free and then derive high-margin revenues from advertising and merchant services distribution."

Filo expresses surprise at how fast and smoothly Yahoo! has grown. "We were in the right place at the right time, and grew the company with the help of fortunate circumstances," he says modestly. With such fast growth, "even if there are bad decisions, your mistakes get absolved and end up being positive. Things that didn't quite work out right get left by the side." Adds investor Moritz: "The wind has been at our backs." In the sprint for the Internet search engine market, Yahoo! hit the starting line about the same time as a number of competitors, but it has since outpaced them all. What it's done right is expand the market by expanding its search engine capability into more lucrative arenas, like Web-based advertising. To extend the metaphor, it's like the miner who stakes a small claim and uses his gold to start a wildly successful hotel, while his fellow miners continue to labor in the gold mines and eventually spend their earnings at his hotel.

■ PICKING THE RIGHT SEGMENT: EXPLOITING POORLY SERVED MARKETS

Right now, in terms of revenue, Cisco Systems and Cross-Worlds Software are worlds apart. Cisco is an established market leader with more than $6 billion in revenue; Cross-Worlds is a start-up just launching its product, and revenues are almost nonexistent. But the two are following similar paths in their market strategy: Each created a technology to serve a perceived need that no established company had addressed adequately, and they did this with the intent of expanding a narrow niche into a huge market. To date, Cisco has succeeded, and CrossWorlds has high hopes.

At CrossWorlds, CEO Katrina Garnett identified a basic business need that was being missed by numerous big companies which had focused singularly on products that used client-server technology. As explained in Chapter 1, CrossWorld's processware unites differing enterprise applications, allowing companies using it to operate seamlessly. Forrester Research, of Cambridge, estimates that Fortune 500 companies spend 30 percent of their information technology budgets on designing, developing, and maintaining interfaces among all of their applications, a finding that certainly gave CrossWorlds a clue to an underlying gold mine.

"CrossWorlds addresses the dire need of integration between these application islands," says Navid Kahangi, the technology company's vice president of engineering. "In five years we're going to be a standard for integration. Everybody's going to be CrossWorlds-connected. Anybody who comes into the market with a client-server application would want to have a connector into CrossWorlds." That's not as simple as it sounds, because CrossWorlds aims to develop off-the-shelf products that can be mixed and matched between a variety of complex applications. Anyone who's ever tried to import data from a word-processing program into a spreadsheet has a basic idea of the difficulty of making different software applications communicate.

"Timing is everything," wrote the Aberdeen Group, a Boston-based technology analysis firm, in a recent report on CrossWorlds. Companies "are grappling with how to bring together their existing product applications as well as integrating those of the next generation. When it comes to serious business system integration, all roads could well lead to CrossWorlds." That's certainly Garnett's intention.

Cisco is a perfect model for this strategy. Venture capitalist Don Valentine, an early investor in Cisco and its chairman during 1986–1995, says the company's primary technology, the router, made sense of a "Tower of Babel"—enabling the different languages that computer networks use for internal communication to talk with each other. Today, more than 80 percent of corporate routers connected to the Internet are Cisco's.

"The first thing we did correctly was find the market and focus on it," says John Morgridge, the current chairman and former CEO who grew the company to the $1 billion mark. The next correct step was being consciously driven by what customers wanted, rather than by what Cisco's engineers might have wanted to design. It sounds simple, but it's still a rarity in high tech. "We were driven to accommodate whatever equipment the customer arrayed in front of us," says Morgridge. "We were not purists; we'd respond to what the customer wanted."

"The first thing we did correctly was find the market and focus on it. This company has never been particularly visionary. We have been very market sensitive."
—John Morgridge, Chairman, Cisco Systems

Meeting customer needs, and leveraging its product through powerful partnerships, account for Cisco's over-whelming domination of a new market. Cisco established early distribution agreements with AT&T, Hewlett-Packard, and Digital Equipment. "We've been very lucky," Morgridge admits. "We hit the sweet spot and grew with it. This company has never been particularly visionary. We have been very market sensitive."

Says Valentine: "Part of Cisco's success was its ability to forge relationships with everyone. They recently announced collaborative partnerships with Intel and Microsoft. They figure out how to do business together, even though they're competing someplace else." Cisco is now that big, fat target that Anderson mentioned earlier; its challenge is to avoid getting complacent and allowing competitors to take away market share with newer products. (See Ascend Communications later in this chapter as an example of someone trying to do just that.) To return to the gold-rush analogy, Cisco has made a big strike and has to fend off the onrush of new claimants.

■ JUMPING A CLAIM

Being the first to launch a product in a new market does not always guarantee success. Once there was a Silicon Valley company, Digital Research, that had the first viable PC operating system, called CP/M. But the man who created CP/M and founded DRI, Gary Kildall, chose not to license the technology to IBM, which wanted to put CP/M on its nascent personal computer. In a story of missed opportunity that has become legend in the industry, Kildall was out flying that day in 1980 when IBM came calling. In his absence, DRI's attorney refused to sign the IBM contract because it appeared to be overly restrictive. Even when Kildall came down to earth and got details of IBM's proposal, he was reluctant to sign over his baby, and the two sides could never agree to terms. What was then another obscure start-up, Microsoft, did respond to IBM's overtures, though it had to buy an operating system from someone else to do it. This became MS-DOS, precursor to Windows—and DRI became nothing but a footnote (long since absorbed into another company). Kildall died tragically in 1994 of injuries sustained when he fell and hit his head in a bar.

"When we talk about getting to the future first, it's not about having the first product launch. . . . There's a huge difference between being first to market and first to leadership."
—Gary Hamel, author of *Competing for the Future*

The Kildall story has its moral: Opportunism can be more important than having the first or even the best technology. "When we talk about getting to the future first, it's not about having the first product launch," says author Gary Hamel. "It's about being the company that learns fast enough and gets to that solid strategic positioning in a big market first. There's a huge difference between being first to market and first to leadership." Consequently, while technology companies and venture capital investors drool at the prospect of first-mover advantage—that is, being first to enter a new market—the knowledgeable ones realize that's only the opening salvo in the battle.

If you're entering a niche that has been established by someone else, it's crucial that you develop a product that is better, faster, cheaper, and more efficient than theirs. Sun Microsystems ousted minicomputer manufacturers like Digital Equipment with workstations that were a fraction of the cost and which sat on the user's desk. PCs equipped with Microsoft's Windows NT are now threatening to do the same to Sun's workstations. This kind of leapfrogging is endemic to the technology industry. It has its dark side—constant upgrades and claims of superior performance that cause beleaguered information systems directors to reach for the Zantac—but the benefit is that no one in the technology industry gets complacent. If you're second to market, "your product has to be a ten-times improvement on the existing product," says the Yankee Group's Anderson. "It does something ten times faster or ten times easier. When you've got that, the market will make way for you."

➤ Shaping and Adapting

McKinsey consultant John Hagel contrasts market shapers, who evangelize and unify a new market, with market adapters, who join the fray later. "As an adapter, the focus is to more finely segment the market, to create a customer segment that's distinctive for your product or service. You have to build capability to move very quickly and cannibalize your product, if necessary." In the technology industry, adapters pour into the market literally overnight; these days, it only takes a few entrepreneurially-minded programmers to convince a venture capitalist that they've got a better mousetrap—and presto, there's competition.

When it comes to technology markets, claim-jumping is an omnipresent possibility. Now let's look at two companies who have attempted it—one is strongly challenging the leader in its segment, and the other has become the leader.

➤ Shooting at the Leader

When Ascend Communications of Alameda, California, was founded in 1989, it didn't really intend to compete with Cisco. It targeted a different niche altogether. But as often happens in the technology industry, products that were once in separate spheres wound up overlapping as new abilities were added to them—a process called *convergence*. Ascend's first product, shipped in 1991, was an integrated hardware-software combination for corporate videoconferencing. Early partners included long-distance providers

EXPERT OPINION

John Hagel III, Principal, McKinsey & Company, Palo Alto. With McKinsey for 13 years; in Silicon Valley office for seven years

On the Forces Shaping High-Tech's Management Style:

"The forces are the extra amount of uncertainty, combined with a high degree of complexity and interdependence. You need to maximize the value of your web. Unless the web succeeds, the company dies. An early strategy question, what web are you going to play in? Are you going to be a hedger or a disciple, as with Netscape or Microsoft? Or do you create your own web?"

On Emerging Management Models:

"There will be different styles. As uncertainty increases, most companies fall back on an adaptive posture—'If I can just stay one step ahead.' Another approach is to figure 'the old truths are no longer correct, this is an opportunity to shape a new future that I can take advantage of.' You embrace uncertainty as an opportunity and shape the future."

On Creating a Market Niche:

"What's critical is creating enough incentives to mobilize other players behind your product. That happens before you launch your product. You shape expectations to the point where people believe that you're going to be the winner. As an adapter the focus is to more finely segment the market, to create a customer segment that's distinctive for your product or service. You have to build capability to move very quickly and cannibalize your product."

(continued)

EXPERT OPINION (Continued)

On Sustaining Growth:

"The more growth you can drive as an enterprise, the more opportunity you create for talented individuals. Stability equals death."

On Customers:

"The most difficult customers are in many ways the most valuable customers. In any marketplace you've got the 80-20 rule. I take a contrarian view and say the really important customers are the five percent who are at the leading edge. They should become partners with you in enhancing the product so that it becomes more valuable."

AT&T, Sprint Corporation, and MCI Communications. As late as the first quarter in 1994, this product accounted for 75 percent of Ascend's revenue.

Then in 1993 came the product enhancements that caused the company to enter a period of hypergrowth: By adding additional functions to a new product dubbed Pipeline Access Server, Ascend gave any company, large or small, the ability to start an Internet business. With the acquisition last year of Cascade Communications, Ascend added a variety of wide-area networking (WAN) products that connect organizations over geographical distances. Meanwhile, the technologies that Cisco, 3Com, and others had developed converged into a broad market called "networking." Since the mid-1990s, Ascend has been playing in Cisco's sandbox.

This heightened competition will severely test Ascend president and CEO Mory Ejabat's drive to win every market he enters. "My motto is put out quality products and always win with respect to your technology, marketing, and salesmanship," Ejabat says. But he acknowledges that, in the overall networking arena, "Cisco definitely is number one, followed by 3Com." He characterizes Ascend's means of differentiation as being the technological leader in offering WAN products aimed at telecommunications carriers and Internet service providers. Cisco's strength is in the corporate enterprise, and 3Com's is in the client and desktop.

Once a market like networking is established, technology matters far less than marketing, brand, and customers. Chip Vetter, managing director of the BancAmerica Robertson Stephens investment bank in San Francisco, explains, "You don't see Cisco as the technology leader; they've become a marketing giant." That's why it won't be easy to wrest market leadership from Cisco. Still, the networking market is so huge and growing so fast that it spawns would-be claim-jumpers galore. These newer entrants come up with technology advances that could, theoretically, thrust them ahead of the market leaders. Cisco and the other big players sometimes buy off the claim-jumpers by absorbing them through an acquisition. Ascend, in fact, recently doubled its size by merging with Cascade. "We've made a decision to be the end-to-end provider of public network solutions, and we're in the last stages of doing that with Cascade," says Ejabat. With its highly visible stock on a perpetual roller coaster, Ascend may be a prime target for acquisition by an even larger company.

■ SELLING YOUR WAY TO THE TOP

Tom Siebel, CEO of Siebel Systems, obviously relishes being a contrarian. He did not have first-mover advantage in his market niche—sales-support software—but he entered the battle with a rush and drove his way to market leadership within about two years after forming his start-up. A consummate salesman himself, Siebel spent seven years at Oracle before leaving to become an entrepreneur. He sold his first company to Oracle competitor Sybase and then used the proceeds to bootstrap Siebel Systems in 1993. We were introduced to Siebel's management style earlier in this book. He runs the company with an iron hand, first operating in extremely lean and mean fashion out of an old brick building in low-rent East Palo Alto.

Siebel needed to run lean and mean—after all, he wasn't exactly starting his company in an uncrowded market. Sales force automation had hundreds of players. A 1996 report by the Gartner Group estimated that more than 1,000 vendors worldwide were attacking some component of the sales function. These were mostly small companies, but the list also included a couple of formidable players, such as Oracle and Lotus (which is now part of IBM). Nonetheless, Siebel smelled opportunity. "What we saw was a reasonably large market segment that was very poorly served by current vendors," Siebel recalls. "It's the classic better mousetrap story. We set out to build a product and a company that met the needs of salespeople." And who should know those needs better than Siebel, who had become the top salesperson at Oracle a year after he joined it.

Siebel assured the effectiveness of his product by pooling his experience with that of his management team and more than 50 customers, including such companies as Bank of America, Wells Fargo, McKesson, Clorox, and Sun Microsystems. The company asked these customers about *their* requirements for sales automation. As Siebel recalls, "We built a product spec, and took it back to our customers and asked them again, 'Is this it? Is this what you want?' "

Siebel Systems is now a $100 million company with close to 50 percent market share in the sales automation niche. It has moved out of the ramshackle building in East Palo Alto to sleek new offices in nearby San Mateo. Siebel says his goal was never to build "insanely great" technology or to make a lot of money, though he's clearly done both. Rather, it was to build a "great, enduring company" which employees could look at with pride and say, "I helped create that."

Siebel, the man and his company, have defined and taken over a market segment by following a simple formula that is too often ignored by technologists: Know your customers, listen to what they want, and respond to that more quickly and more precisely than your competitors. Dawn Lepore, chief information officer of Charles Schwab Corporation, says that using Siebel's products allows the retail brokerage to handle more transactions faster and give greater customer service. Schwab likes the products so much that it has a testimonial letter posted on Siebel's Web site.

■ ANOTHER PLANET HEARD FROM: THE ALTRUISTIC ENTREPRENEUR

What happens when you enter a market with the altruistic notion of bettering society? Can that coincide with financial success? Tenth Planet Explorations, a California technology company, is staking its future on the answers to these questions. Although financial rewards remain a future uncertainty, the four-year-old company has already succeeded in penetrating its market, elementary school education, with its multimedia software product. Located outside of mainstream Silicon Valley in offbeat Half Moon Bay, Tenth Planet's headquarters presents a starkly different image than do utilitarian business software companies like Siebel's. Inside, kites and children's drawings adorn the whitewashed walls—the company clearly has gotten to know its customers. That feeling is also embodied in its name. "We liked 'Tenth Planet' because it implies exploring and discovering," says founder and CEO Cheryl Vedoe, who left Apple's education division to start the company in 1994. "If you had a tenth planet you could make that world the way you wanted it to be."

Although Tenth Planet has an idealistic goal—enhancing the traditional elementary school curriculum with software programs that make learning more accessible—Vedoe says bluntly that "I wouldn't have started the company if I didn't believe we could make money. I'm a businessperson. I saw a business opportunity that was consistent with my personal goal to continue to participate in this market, even if the market was a little slow to develop." Regarding that latter situation, she notes that while the United States spends $300 billion annually on K–12 education, only a small percentage of that goes to technology. Opening up that market to technology has proven to be a daunting task that is going to take years more of commitment and effort.

"It's a challenging market," Vedoe admits. "The most important thing we have to do to succeed is to deliver sound instruction through our products. We want to help schools with technology in a meaningful way through core instruction. The ultimate proof is to show improvements in test scores and outcomes." She says selling to schools must be done by relying on the slow process of word-of-mouth. School boards must be convinced to adopt the products and teachers persuaded to use them. Both boards and teachers like to hear from peers who have already used the products. 1997 was Tenth Planet's first complete school year with products in the market. These included a series of programs designed to help children increase their understanding of math concepts with interactive software, hands-on activities, and Internet resources. "You need a full school year to start creating awareness," says Vedoe.

Another approach that differentiates Tenth Planet's products from business or consumer software is that the company deliberately does not offer the latest, fastest, and greatest in multimedia applications, because schools typically do not have the hardware to support it. "We have a customer base that may not be ready to accept all the technological innovation we could deliver," says Vedoe. "We have to strike a balance. Our customer base doesn't have broad-based access to the leading-edge technology. We want to be innovative in our approach to teaching, in terms of the lessons we define, and how we use the range of media available to us, both technology and print."

Penetrating the education market requires an extended ramping-up period, and the payoff period can be just as long. "Education customers are intensely loyal once you establish your market," says Vedoe, noting that besieged Apple, while struggling in other arenas, still owns half the education market. "If they trust you, they'll buy your next product and your next." Tenth Planet is working hard to develop that trust by establishing itself as a patient company committed to a cause, not just to return on investment.

➤ "A Social Experiment"

Another example of a cause driving a product is First Virtual Corporation (FVC), founded in 1993 by third-time entrepreneur Ralph Ungermann. At 55, Ungermann is older than most technology executives, but what he's doing at Santa Clara–based FVC belies the notion that only the young have radical ideas. One observer calls FVC a social experiment more than a company because it was structured under Ungermann's notions of open environments, outsourcing, and cross-fertilization. Indeed, before he figured out what market he wanted to enter, Ungermann knew how he wanted to structure the company. "When I started the company, the only thing I focused on was the architecture of the company, not products, technology, or markets," he says. "I wanted something more compatible with the way I do things. I never enjoyed managing a large organization."

Except for a few conference rooms off to the side, FVC's office is one large room filled with desks pushed close together in pods. Nearly all the employees work, talk, and eat out in the open. "There are only two people in our company that aren't on this floor," says Ungermann. "We have 50 people and everybody's in the open. There's random location seating." He got the idea from the trading floor of stock exchanges. "People will yell across the room when they need information." If you want to block out the noise, you use headsets and earphones. As in a family situation, FVC's employees might argue a lot, but they settle issues quickly and don't hold grudges. "It's very hard for a problem or a success to go unnoticed. The information flow is quicker."

Most companies pick their product and their market before they build a culture, but Ungermann did it the other way. FVC's product line—software aimed at enabling high-quality video over corporate intranets—grew directly out of his emphasis on open communications. Ungermann's idea is to link the corporate world via asynchronous transfer mode (ATM) switching, which boosts the ability of fiber-optic lines to carry data and so far has been used primarily in the telecommunications industry. Like Ascend's Ejabat, he believes that existing solutions are inadequate. "Entrenched video networking left a lot to be desired," says Ungermann. "We have an incredibly wide range of products in video networking; we have competitors in each section but we tie them all together as a system." (FVC uses its own technology to run the company. For example, during our meeting Ungermann took a video phone call from Steelcase, a customer that was about to start running the FVC system throughout the corporation. Interestingly, Steelcase pioneered alternative work space designs through its furniture products and consulting service.)

"The best way to create a competitive company is to focus on speed and leverage—time to market, time to change," says Ungermann. "We architected a company that had the best chance of moving fast." In other words, he bred a racehorse and then looked around for a race to run it in. "I want to create another real market segment, in this case video networking, and dominate it," he says. Most of his peers in the industry remain skeptical as to whether what's essentially a product built on a culture can be successful.

VIEW FROM THE TOP

Perspectives from Tim Koogle, CEO, Yahoo! Incorporated

On the Internet versus Traditional High Tech:

"The rate of change is a lot higher for Internet-based companies than for just about any other high-tech area. It is one of the things that attracted me. There was also the fact that there were no rules at the outset. The business models had not been set and there was an unprecedented rate of growth in user adoption as well as predicted dollars being spent in advertising and e-commerce."

On Managing People and Sustaining Growth:

"I learned a long time ago how to let go. You can't let your ego get in the way. The only way to scale a high-growth company is to hire people who are smarter and better in their specialty than you are, get clear about what it is they will do, stay accessible so that they can constantly hear the direction you have set, and then get out of the way. We have done this from the beginning here at Yahoo! We are constantly pushing decisions down in the organization."

On Innovation:

"We have no lack of that here at Yahoo! We religiously set the company's strategy and overall operational objectives and then push the authority to make decisions about how to execute down in the organization. We've also kept the bar really high in hiring smart and aggressive people. The end result is hundreds of people inventing new ways to compete every day."

(continued)

VIEW FROM THE TOP (Continued)

On Winning Mind Share:

"From the outset, we thought of our company as an information delivery or media business. Ask any executive in a well-run media business what is important and they will tell you: brand, quality content, and distribution. We have focused on this short list from the start. A strong brand gets you to the top of the consumer's mind, distribution keeps them bumping into you, and quality content is the experience that keeps them coming back."

On Customers:

"We have an interesting business with essentially two customer bases: one that doesn't pay (our global consumer audience who accesses our service for free), and one that does (our large set of international advertisers and merchant services providers). We pay a lot of attention to both. We get thousands of e-mails every day from both sets of customers giving us input on what they think we've done right as well as suggestions for what they think we haven't done so well. We also have a rapidly growing sales force that's in touch with our customers daily. All of that input is routed into the company directly to the producers in charge of making and improving our products as well as into the sales operations group."

On Alliances:

"We are huge believers in partnering on every level. Things change and move so rapidly in our industry that it would be impossible to succeed without it. We have hundreds of contractual partnerships worldwide that span the areas of

(continued)

VIEW FROM THE TOP (Continued)

content, distribution, merchant and communication services, and technology. We also have begun to make selective acquisitions over the past several months. I had a rule that we were not going to acquire anyone else's business until we had proved to ourselves and our shareholders that we could consistently run our own. But we have done that and we are beginning to selectively make important acquisitions as a way of further fueling our strategy."

On Structure at Yahoo!:

"I have already mentioned our approach in hiring really smart people and pushing authority to make decisions down in the organization. We run an extremely flat organization with minimal management overhead. We are functionally organized with cross-functional teams that are formed quickly to launch new products and then dissolved quickly to go on to the next one."

On Minimizing Turnover:

"I have been amazed at the lack of turnover here at Yahoo! We currently have about 600 people and since we started the company we have probably lost about 10. I would attribute it to several factors. The first is that people have the very real sense that what we are creating has no limits. It is changing the world. Second, people always want to win and to work at a leading company. Knock on wood (yes, I am superstitious and paranoid!)—they see that in Yahoo! Third, there is a huge number of smart people here who are fun to work with. Last, we have been very strongly dedicated to making everyone an owner of the company through liberal stock options. Everyone in the company has them and we give renewal grants every year."

■ THE BOTTOM LINE

From the examples presented in this chapter, it's obvious that there is no one best way of establishing or entering a market. The technology industry has become far more complex than in the early 1980s, when a company like Microsoft could quickly build up near-monopolistic dominance on the basis of one licensing deal with IBM. Technological change is continuing at such a rapid pace that new niches are constantly being created and technologists keep on finding new ways to slice and dice their markets. The result, claims Internet analyst Daniel H. Rimer of the San Francisco investment bank Hambrecht & Quist LLC, is that "technology has become less important than the actual ability to communicate what your product or service is."

As much of the technology industry moves from a revolutionary into an evolutionary stage, the goal is to better serve existing markets by improving response time, boosting bandwidth, and creating greater connectivity. Hence, the carefully targeted approaches of CrossWorlds, Siebel Systems, and Ascend. In some ways, that's a tougher assignment than simply attacking a brand-new opportunity.

For one thing, you've got to defeat or go around the players who are already in your niche. And they started the same way you did, so they're not going to be blind to what you're doing for long. "From Microsoft to Cisco to Intel, you're seeing a lot of paranoia," says Rimer. "The entrepreneurs of the last wave are now established companies trying to defend market share against the new wave." Adds headhunter David Powell: "You can't make a mistake when you're up against the established niche. You've got to make a swift, lethal launch—so quick and agile in your penetration that it will take a while for someone to catch up. Otherwise, they'll see you coming and the big guys will squash you."

However, meaningful innovation that changes the way we do things is still possible. Rimer's comments above are a bit glib; technology is important and breakthroughs happen. The emergence of the Internet as a mass medium for communication and interaction has spawned a multitude of start-ups who want to take advantage of this new world. They sometimes reach back toward old models and reconfigure them for the Internet, as Yahoo! did in reaping revenue via advertising and content aggregation. We are witnessing the creation of companies that exist only because of the Internet, such as Firefly or Amazon.com, but at the same time the Internet is transforming the way pre-Internet technology companies do business. Cisco, for example, sells billions of dollars worth of products and services via the Web, while PeopleSoft offers extensive customer service and training there.

You could say the Internet is the second great wave in the era that began with the introduction of the PC and the microprocessor. In a way, the Internet is bringing us back together after the stand-alone PC made each of us a separate little work center. Finding markets that exploit these kinds of sea changes is an exciting, perilous process.

"In these unpredictable arenas you learn how to operate as close to the uncertainties as possible without being overwhelmed by them," says UC Berkeley professor Raymond Miles. "You're trying to reach deeper into a knowledge pool without drowning. You're awash in a sea of knowledge and simply trying to stay afloat." The best way to stay afloat is to create a market that you know more about than anybody else—amounting to a claim you can defend.

Chapter

Mind Share Is a Terrible Thing to Waste

It's clear from the tone of communications between Silicon Valley and Washington, D.C., these days that there's no love lost between technology executives and politicians. Technology executives are known for their libertarian views—exhibiting a general disdain for government regulation or involvement in their freewheeling industry. Bill Gates' sneering response to the Department of Justice's antitrust lawsuit against Microsoft sums up the general attitude. For their part, most politicians (except for high-tech groupies like the president and vice president) regard technology with suspicion. The U.S. Senate even bars members from bringing laptop computers onto the floor out of fear that the machines might prove disruptive. But though they don't understand each other, techno-execs and politicos share one important trait: In both arenas, success depends upon well-orchestrated campaigns. To launch themselves and their products, technology companies spend considerable sums on external public relations consultants and lavish events designed to impress critical thought leaders like journalists and industry analysts. The epitome of such events is the massive spectacle called Comdex, the technology industry's annual three-ring circus of a trade show in Las Vegas.

Why all the hoopla? *Mind share.* More than ever, perception precedes reality in today's high-tech arena. What people believe about a company and its products—where it rates on the mind share scale—is vital to future success. Intel is an acknowledged master of mind share manipulation, convincing millions that they must have "Intel inside" their PC to have the highest-quality machine, even though competing chips are very nearly identical in functionality and performance.

For a company, gaining mind share involves splashing itself across a host of media, from TV programs devoted to high-tech gadgetry to magazines that cover the latest trends and culture of the cyber-savvy. Technology companies foster awareness of their market positioning and their products through a variety of techniques, including wooing key analysts at firms such as Forrester Research and the Yankee Group, winning over journalists in business and trade media, providing glitzy demonstrations and appearances in conferences and trade shows, proclaiming their product a "standard" that others must follow, and—the favorite—defining themselves as a "market leader" even when the market barely exists.

"Differentiating your product from others is more important than having the better product," proclaims Paul Franson, a longtime Silicon Valley marketing consultant and author (*High Tech, High Hope,* John Wiley & Sons, 1998). Trade shows such as Comdex and Internet World generate excitement and headlines. As the technology industry becomes increasingly consumerized, even business-to-business products are promoted like consumer products. "You sell to the information systems department with the buzz surrounding your reputation," says Franson.

Because of the speed at which new products are developed, particularly those involving the Internet, companies can't afford to wait until they have their product ready to ship or even off the drawing board before seeking mind share. What CrossWorlds did through its launch party was to sell a notion—processware—because an actual product wouldn't appear for another five months.

"Mind share happens before you have a product out," says investment banker Chip Vetter. High-tech products are difficult for customers to differentiate so they make decisions based on reputations. "It starts at the earliest stages—blowing your horn in conferences and PR campaigns before you go public." *Forbes* magazine's Eric Nee compares the technology industry to the fashion industry. "It runs on image. You've got to put on a show, unveil the new fashions."

Venture capitalist Ann Winblad has another metaphor: technology as seduction—of analysts, customers, partners, investors. "You have to start the seduction process when you're getting a company going. You want to make sure that there are dogs willing to eat the dog food," she notes, utilizing a common though unpalatable saying from the technology industry. Her firm, Hummer Winblad Venture Partners, requires would-be entrepreneurs who are seeking an infusion of capital to visit potential customers and demonstrate what the company is trying to do. Even without products, this phase is a good test of an entrepreneur's ability to work an audience. Today, a technology entrepreneur must be more showman than technician, able to conjure up the sizzle before the steak's even hit the grill.

■ CULTIVATING THE INFLUENCERS

Every industry has opinion leaders whose comments can make or break a product and a company. In high tech, there are two reigning influential forces: the trade press— the hundreds of magazines, newspapers, and newsletters that follow every niche you can think of, from microprocessors to Internet tools—and the industry analysts—who specialize in making recommendations on new products for end users. (Industry analysts, who issue their reports by market segment, are not to be confused with financial analysts. Industry analysts assess technology from both public and private companies for the benefit of corporate audiences; financial analysts, employed by brokerage houses and investment banks, report on companies and market segments, but tend to focus on publicly traded entities. Their "buy" recommendations are for stock, not technology.)

Even as start-ups, technology companies "must be able to manage the media and analysts," sums up Rick Sherlund, managing director with investment bank Goldman Sachs & Company in New York. Consumers and corporations rely on these experts to interpret technology for them.

PeopleSoft knew it had arrived when the Gartner Group listed it as a market leader in the enterprise applications arena, along with SAP AG. "We've got mind share with the buyer, vis-à-vis the Gartner Group," exults PeopleSoft CEO Dave Duffield. "We and SAP are listed as the leaders. Any big company will check the Gartner Group if they're going to buy enterprise software. Opinion makers are buying our products."

Two other key opinion makers are market researchers Dataquest and International Data Corporation (IDC), whose projections on the growth of market segments, no matter how unsupported, are widely quoted by the press and companies themselves. Every time a company issues a press release, it tries to include a projection on the size of its market. Journalists seize on these numbers, which make ready fodder for headlines about the latest billion-dollar technology market.

The Internet adds a new dimension to the mind share mix. Technology companies are now able to interact directly with user groups and customers to champion products, offer information and fixes for product flaws, and, increasingly, make sales. Company Internet sites are also accessed routinely by journalists and analysts seeking information.

The processes that high-tech companies use to solicit support and gain greater visibility offer valuable lessons for nontechnology companies. Whatever their field, companies can utilize the techniques cited in this chapter to identify the opinion leaders in their industry and strengthen their own marketing efforts.

■ BEING THE MARKET LEADERS

One way to generate mind share is to be identified as *the* market leader. Check Point Software Technologies, introduced earlier in this book, routinely refers to itself as the leader in its niche—protecting corporate Internet sites from unwanted intrusion, by means of electronic firewalls. As evidence, it cites a 1996 Yankee Group report which states that Check Point has 44 percent of the firewall market, versus 13 percent for the nearest competitor. Yankee Group's report, which drew from the first half of 1996 to assemble figures, identified the total firewall market as being precisely 9,109 units. Check Point had sold just over 4,000 units to lay claim to market leadership—and over half of those had been sold through one vendor, Sun Microsystems, which bundled Check Point's firewall with its own powerful computers.

"It wasn't very meaningful," confesses Check Point CEO Deb Triant, but it had tremendous impact. "We had a study that showed we were the market leader, and made a very aggressive effort to get across that message. We took our 44 percent market share and put that on the Web site." Incidentally, the same Yankee Group report showed that Check Point had a far less impressive 27 percent market share by revenue, out of a total market of $45 million.

This is not to discredit Check Point or the Yankee Group. On the contrary, Check Point's identification as a market leader is a textbook example of what every emerging technology company wants to do. With a strong marketing campaign that paraded the 44 percent market share number through the business and trade press, and in the company's promotional material, Check Point gained increasing mind share because anyone doing an article or researching Internet security had to make a requisite phone call to the market leader. Thanks to the Yankee Group report and the resulting publicity Check Point was able to generate, the company emerged as being the clearly visible leader, and that became self-reinforcing.

"The name of this game is market share and market penetration."

—Deb Triant, CEO, Check Point Software Technologies

Industry expert and author Geoff James seconds the notion: "The absolutely key thing is to establish yourself as a player before anyone else. Otherwise, you can get lost in the noise." Any chief information officer at a Fortune 500 company will tell you that the safest approach is to buy from the market leader, even if that "market leader" has only sold 4,000 units. The assumption is that the market leader will be a long-term survivor while other competitors might fade away.

➤ "We Wrote the Book on It"

Tom Siebel, founder and CEO of Siebel Systems, took an unusual route to achieving mind share. "We wanted to establish ourselves as having intellectual leadership in the market," says Siebel. Looking around for examples, he noticed how that had been done by Charles Schwab, founder of the nation's largest discount brokerage company, based in nearby San Francisco. Schwab, a member of Siebel Systems' board of directors, had written a rather self-serving book, *How to Be Your Own Stockbroker,* in which he touted the advantages of investing without paying the hefty fees of the full-service brokerages that were Schwab's competition. "We patterned ourselves after Charles Schwab," says Siebel. "We wanted to become thought leaders in sales force automation. So we wrote the book on it, literally."

Published by Free Press in 1994, a year after the founding of Siebel Systems, *Virtual Selling: Going Beyond the Automated Sales Force to Achieve Total Sales Quality* established Siebel as a player. Coauthored by Michael Malone, a well-known technology journalist, *Virtual Selling* described how sales force automation software must be incorporated within an overall philosophy that supports the sales force in new ways.

In the book, Siebel covers the strategies of customer-driven products, empowered teams, and a flattened, entrepreneurial structure and discusses how they are applied to his own company. "We give customers a chance to buy our software from the people who wrote the book on sales automation," Siebel says. "It was absolutely not an ego trip. It was all marketing. We had some things we wanted to communicate and we were establishing a leadership position." Siebel has handed out hundreds of copies to customers, analysts, and journalists. The book even garnered a favorable review in *Booklist,* the review journal of the American Library Association.

To further strengthen the company's leadership position, Siebel started a trade show devoted to sales force automation, giving the plenary keynote in November 1994. Today that conference, the DCI Sales Force Automation Conference and Exposition, is held in five regional locations in the United States and Canada each year, and attended by 25,000 people. Siebel continues to give the keynote address at every show. With the titles of author, trade show host, and speaker added to CEO, salesman, and entrepreneur, Siebel has most of the mind share bases covered.

➤ The Power of Controversy: Selling Online Erotica

One way to capture customers' attention is by selling something that's unique, newsworthy, and controversial. Of course, nothing gains more attention than being embroiled in a juicy controversy. And what's juicier than sex? NetNoir is a three-year-old San Francisco–based start-up whose name is its message: It aims to be the leading new media company focused on Afrocentric content. (*Noir* is a French word for black, as in film *noir.*) CEO E. David Ellington decided that to fully serve its audience, NetNoir needed to add a "Black Erotica" section to its sites on America Online (AOL) and the Web. Obviously, this was a controversial decision given the content. Even within NetNoir itself, there was some doubt. "It was a business decision," Ellington says. "There's e-mail, financial information, news, sports, and sex. I said we're going to build the erotica site on the Web and charge for it." The notoriety this decision brought increased NetNoir's visibility and mind share. And because the site is not hard-core, it has managed to get advertising. The lengthy intro to NetNoir's erotica site (which is actually directed by a woman) talks about presenting "as many aspects of our diverse culture as we possibly can . . . Our audience has expressed a desperate need for such a forum, to showcase 'true' examples of erotica as it exists within African-American culture."

Black Erotica and NetNoir's position as one of the few black-themed sites on the Web have helped generate considerable publicity. In 1995, NetNoir's executives did an interview and photo session that appeared on the front of the business section in the *San Francisco Examiner.* "That was truly serendipitous because the Net really exploded in early '95, and everybody was saying, 'What about minorities?,' " Ellington remembers. *Fortune* picked NetNoir as one of its "25 Cool Companies." There were articles in *Le Monde,* the *New York Times,* and the *Wall Street Journal,* and others distributed by the Associated Press. With all of the press coverage and a $1 million investment from partner AOL, "that gave us validity," Ellington adds. "It gave the stamp of approval for the white folks."

Things snowballed from there. After the Black Erotica site was mentioned in the *New York Times,* Ellington attended a technology conference with Vice President Al Gore. "Gore took off his glasses, looked at me, and said, 'I just read a lot about this company,' " Ellington recalls. "He had a twinkle in his eye. So I said, 'I'm glad to see that as vice president you're well informed. But that's only one aspect of our company.' " Ellington was also invited to the prestigious G7 economics conference in South Africa. And then the big kahuna itself, Microsoft, formed a joint venture with Black Entertainment Television (BET) in January 1996 to coproduce an interactive Web site (www.msbet .com) devoted to black issues. "People said, 'There must be an African-American market or Microsoft wouldn't even think about it,' " Ellington recalls. Clearly, NetNoir had a legitimate niche, and now mind share galore.

Ellington has emerged as a spokesman for African-American causes in the online community. It's a role the articulate former lawyer seems comfortable with. "Brand is everything in our business," he says. "We're the number-one black brand in cyberspace."

➤ Selling Diversity

Technology companies aren't the first to exploit diversity, of course. But companies like NetNoir are proving that, especially in the online world, the ability to define your company's image with laser-like precision is a major factor in the fight for winning mind share. And that image can be multifaceted. Some people know NetNoir only through Black Erotica; others access its sports or media or news sites.

"The Net can be a very powerful medium to capture mind share."

—John Hagel, author of *Net.Gain*

By expanding the model, any company can hone a facet of its image through the creation of an online community that helps establish it as an expert in that area. Pharmaceutical companies, for instance, can set up sites devoted to diseases for which they offer treatments, thereby presenting themselves as both compassionate and cutting-edge. "The Net can be a very powerful medium to capture mind share," says McKinsey consultant John Hagel. "With the Net you've got access to real-time ongoing focus groups."

■ FIND PARTNERS YOU CAN BANK ON!

If controversy isn't your cup of tea and you don't have the time to write a book, find a great partner with mind share of its own. For many years, VeriFone, based in Redwood City, was literally the obscure black box behind the curtain when it came to financial transactions. The company was the leading manufacturer of transaction authorization systems—those omnipresent little boxes that retailers use to verify credit-card transactions—but was almost unknown in its own right. It had market share, but no mind share. Now it's stepping out from behind the curtain to become a dominant force in the much broader market of electronic commerce (e-commerce). VeriFone has done this by expanding its product line, offering a consumer product that allows people in their homes to pay bills through electronic cash transactions. Hewlett-Packard, the nation's second-largest technology company after IBM, thought enough of VeriFone's prospects in this potentially huge market to pay $1.4 billion a year ago to make it a wholly owned subsidiary.

With HP's backing, CEO Hatim Tyabji* is making an aggressive effort to transform VeriFone into a consumer

---

*Tyabji announced plans to retire at the end of 1998.

company. But to do this, Verifone must get the attention of customers, potential partners, and competitors. It needs mind share. One way to gain this visibility is by leveraging HP. Says Tyabji: "HP has done a marvelous job of becoming ubiquitous in the consumer's mind. And our strategy in e-commerce means consumer systems. HP has mind share and channels. We're launching a very aggressive, embryonic foray into consumer products and we aim to learn from HP." E-commerce is expected to be a huge market within the next several years, but the $64 million question is when? While the vendors wait for the market to take off, says Tyabji, "We've got to continue to make huge investments without knowing when they'll pay off. With HP we've got deep pockets."

Since Tyabji took over in 1986, VeriFone has grown from $31.2 million in sales to $600 million in 1997. In mind share, however, VeriFone trailed far behind much smaller companies. Tyabji was content with that. "What I didn't want," he says, "was to emulate a number of Silicon Valley companies who generate an image before they have anything else." A rarity in the industry, VeriFone succeeded sans mind share because it provided the product, while its customers, notably the major credit card companies and banks, supplied the sizzle. "We hid our light under a bushel," Tyabji says, but as the company began pursuing new markets in the highly publicized e-commerce arena, "we realized our lack of image was hurting us." So the company decided to take the light out from under the bushel. "We're a very substantive company with a very successful track record. We weren't some start-up trying to figure out what the hell to do," he says crisply.

Tyabji's dream is nothing less than to make obsolete the automated teller machine (ATM) as it exists today. "We will move the ATM from a brick and mortar building to your kitchen," he explains. In late 1997, in conjunction with Citicorp, VeriFone launched the PATM (personal ATM), a small gray box that resides in people's homes. Connected to any standard telephone line, it utilizes a smart card to make virtual cash transactions from your account to anywhere—the electric company or the supermarket or the department store. You can also make purchases over the Internet or interact with other online merchants. VeriFone is creating a larger presence for itself by ensuring that both its name and Citicorp's are on the machines, which Tyabji hopes will become as widespread as retail transaction boxes. "As these devices start going into people's homes, we're hopeful our name will become more known to consumers," he says. "We want the mind share." In an earlier product line created for financial institutions, VeriFone made the boxes but Wells Fargo & Co. was the name that went on them. "I made that mistake once; I'm not going to do it again," Tyabji says. "We should have put our name on it. We were just stupid."

Amid the numerous start-ups attempting to exploit the Internet, VeriFone is an exception. It is a venerable, experienced company founded in 1981, with well-established products, profitability, and a strong revenue flow. Without downplaying the strong support of powerful Hewlett-Packard, one can safely cite VeriFone as proof that an established but "demure" company can exploit opportunities to solidify market attention, or mind share.

■ BE AN AUTHORITY—CREATE A STANDARD

In addition to rewriting the rules of business, the technology industry is rewriting our language, or at least expanding it by way of creating an industry "standard." Once *standard* meant a well-established rule or custom, such as standard English (which itself has been undermined by cyberculture and e-mail). What *standard* formally means in the technology industry, however, is "agreed-upon specifications that allow hardware and software to work together." Any software developer who is writing to the Windows standard knows that the software will be compatible with the vast majority of personal computers (except for Apple's Macintosh machines). The http standard, or hyptertext transport protocol, allows anyone who surfs the Web to link documents across millions of sites. Standards can be owned by individual companies, such as Windows by Microsoft, or enforced by a standards committee such as the International Standards Organization (ISO).

"Microsoft had a standard other companies could develop around. In an emerging field, you've got to get together and come up with a common standard."
—Joe K. Carter, Andersen Consulting

To a technology company, either promulgating a standard or becoming part of one is like raising a banner on a hillside that says, "I've arrived." It signifies that you're part of a growing community. You may compete with other members of the community at one level, but you also work with them to advance your standard over someone else's. The Apple-Microsoft battle centered on the latter's willingness to make Windows a standard for PC clones, while Apple kept its Macintosh operating system confined to its proprietary hardware. "You need a collaborative model," points out Andersen Consulting's Joe Carter. "The difference between Microsoft and Apple has nothing to do with technology. Microsoft had a standard other companies could develop around. In an emerging field, you've got to get together and come up with a common standard."

Ideally, what any company would like to do is proclaim itself as the champion of a new standard. Check Point, for example, is promoting a network security standard called the Open Platform for Secure Enterprise Connectivity, or OPSEC. "We're moving from the firewall market into the enterprise security market," says CEO Triant. "The firewall puts up a safety valve for one Internet connection, but a company's problem today is much bigger: multiple connections, internal nets. With OPSEC we're creating a framework for managing security across the entire enterprise." In other words, having OPSEC as a standard enables a company to create similar security across differing technologies. It also lets Check Point, which is already calling itself a market leader, announce that it has created a standard the industry is following.

Used properly, a standard is much bigger than just technological specifications. In the hands of a skilled mind share practitioner, it becomes a philosophical proclamation of where you stand on an issue that just happens to be drawing a lot of attention. Content providers and electronic publishers rally behind the standard of a free and open Internet, protesting government efforts to criminalize online child pornography. Firefly Network, introduced earlier in this book, cocreated the Open Profiling Standard (OPS), designed to allow the online exchange of information between individuals and businesses while still protecting individual privacy. To support this standard, Firefly enlisted "big guns"—including two of the dominant Internet players, Microsoft and Netscape Communications. Today, OPS is under review by an Internet standards body.

"OPS is something we've thought about ever since the company was founded, but we couldn't do it ourselves," explains Firefly CEO Nick Grouf. "We were just too small." He adds that other companies are jumping on the OPS bandwagon because "it speaks to an incredibly powerful social revolution. In a post-OPS world, when I share information with another business, that information belongs to me as an individual. They can't share it without my permission." And here's the numbers game again: After Firefly proposed OPS, the Boston Consulting Group predicted that the existence of such a standard would help propel electronic commerce to $12 billion by 2000. So Firefly has grabbed another prerequisite for mind share: a multibillion-dollar market projection.

"You have to embody the metaphor of what you do," Grouf maintains. "We would argue that Firefly is the metaphor for personalization and community on the Net. You also have to be the firm that sets standards—OPS is a classic example of this." Because of this, there has been much more interest in Firefly. In fact, Firefly testified before the Federal Trade Commission in online consumer privacy hearings in June 1997. A few weeks later, the company participated in the conference that unveiled President Clinton's July 1, 1997 Electronic Commerce Initiative. "I was invited down to the White House to talk about the impact of e-commerce, little Firefly alongside IBM, Microsoft, and Netscape. Bill Clinton knows about Firefly," Grouf boasts. Setting standards, then, enables small companies to make an impact far beyond their size, even reaching beyond the boundaries of the high-tech industry.

■ THE NEXT GENERATION OF MIND SHARE: ENTER THE INTERNET

The techniques described in this chapter—establishing yourself as the market leader, becoming the spokesperson for a cause, or creating a standard—have been honed over the past decade into a very complex strategy for succeeding amid fierce competition. Yet such widespread acceptance is the prelude to cannibalization. If everyone has mind share or is vying to get it, then how can the individual company differentiate itself? Geoffrey Moore, no mind share slouch with his famed "crossing the chasm" metaphor, warns that the techniques of appealing to trade press and industry analysts, combined with trade show appearances and consumer advertising, "have been so assimilated that they're losing their ability to be effective."

Katrina Garnett, the CEO of CrossWorlds Software, whose launch was described in Chapter 1, agrees with Moore. So she's turned to another mind share resource: customers. Besides the industry analysts and trade press, early adopters of technology make up another group of influencers whose attention companies compete for. For example, one of CrossWorlds' early adopters is Bay Networks—a connection that is duly noted in numerous CrossWorlds press releases. "Everybody watches what Bay does," says Garnett. By identifying early adopters and building a bridge to them, they can help refine both your marketing techniques and your product.

Yet another way to build mind share is via the Web. CrossWorlds is educating potential customers and partners about its products with online demonstrations. It also edited the videotape of its launch and posted it on its Web site, thereby serving the dual functions of customer support and public relations. Nearly all technology companies have their own Web sites, which serve many constituencies—employees, customers, investors, the public, and the press. "One thing the Internet has done is to allow companies to bypass channels and reach customers directly," notes venture capitalist Jim Breyer. "Previously it was extremely costly and time-intensive to do that." Now, instead of fighting for shelf space in overcrowded retail stores, manufacturers of multimedia software can offer a demo on their Web site, then ship the product based on an online order. Using the Internet as a sales channel means companies can launch their products ever more quickly, wherever they see an opportunity, further advancing the development cycle and adding a new dimension to gaining mind share.

■ THE BOTTOM LINE

In the high-tech industry, the concept of mind share means thinking about image and branding even before product development. Competition is heating up in all sectors of the economy, and if you don't get there first, you may never catch up—even with a better product. Or, at the least, extensive and expensive efforts will be required.

EXPERT OPINION

Regis McKenna, founder of The McKenna Group, and author of *Real Time* and *Relationship Marketing*

On Structure:

As you get bigger you have to get structured. You can't act like a small company when you're a big company. Competition and stock ownership keeps the excitement going. You're in it because you're an owner and you want to go public and make a lot of money. As you get bigger that same excitement prevails—except you now have the tools to make communication much more pervasive. In the early days, 1960s and 1970s, Intel or Apple in Europe was very different than here. Today communication is hourly."

On the Major Forces Driving High Tech:

"The key thing in the high-tech industry is the continual cauldron of competitive pressure. When you collapse U.S. competitiveness into a company of 20 people and offer a prize of extreme wealth, you create an environment highly tuned to success."

On Motivation:

"People start businesses to go public. Everyone starts out to run their own company; the venture community insists on an exit strategy."

On Relationships:

"Alliances, competition, and customers equal development. Those three are what drive product development. Alliances are a risk-reducing factor. A decade ago it was the uniqueness of the product. [There's] no such thing as

(continued)

EXPERT OPINION (Continued)

unique product today. Uniqueness comes in building an infrastructure that sets the standard."

On Mind Share:

"Mind share is strictly to raise money, not get customers. Apple has the greatest mind share in the industry. Mind share comes as a result of products. Young companies think mind share comes first and that's a mistake. You build the infrastructure from beta sites, ISVs, system integrators, distributors, financial analysts, press, and public. If you do the mind share thing and you don't have the infrastructure, you go out of business. Building the infrastructure, no matter how small a company is, takes years. It took Intel and Microsoft 20 years to evolve a profitable model."

"In high tech there are specific institutions that have developed to allow you to get mind share and allegiance very quickly," notes GeoPartners' consultant Jim Moore. Industry gatherings allow the industry to speak to, and about, itself. They have become institutions unto themselves, which serious customers and industry watchers are compelled to attend. Every industry has such institutions, be they gatherings of car dealers, restaurateurs, or union members. Package yourself and your company the way you would a product, and sell it through the following mind share channels.

While the product is still on the drawing board, think about who the key influencers will be in winning acceptance. These are not necessarily end users, but people who act as expert commentators or thought leaders. Sunbeam's attempt to secure the American Medical Association as an endorser of its medical products, though shelved following a storm of criticism from the physician community, at least showed an awareness of this concept. Be imaginative in your endorsement efforts—don't just go for the nearest celebrity. One thing the technology industry has shown is that, particularly with complicated products, consumers and business buyers alike respond to someone with credibility, who has run lab tests or used the product, or has expert knowledge. Identify conference attendees or user groups for whom the product would be relevant. Technology companies have proven that it's better to focus your attention on the highest level of user, like an HP, and let the word spread.

Find a way to differentiate your company among the diverse groups to whom the product will appeal. Don't craft a one-size-fits-all campaign. The Internet and other online services such as AOL offer an ideal means to send precise messages tailored to particular groups. They are creating communities of shared interests where potential customers can instantaneously obtain word-of-mouth recommendations. And this does not apply only to technology products: Online user groups and chat areas have sprung up around everything from breast cancer to pet care.

If possible, become a spokesperson for a cause related to your product, as Firefly and Check Point have done in the privacy and security arenas. Another example is Intel's activity on behalf of legal immigration, which it needs to supply the company with skilled workers. It helps if you can find a "standard" for others to rally around, not merely a technological one but a moral imperative that draws people together. Chemical and pharmaceutical companies sound the alarm over declines in scientific spending for research, opening the door for their message about the importance and cost of their own privately funded discovery efforts. Leading health maintenance organizations recently called on the government to establish minimum standards of care that all must provide.

Don't be afraid of controversy. Most companies shy away from getting involved in anything controversial, hid-ing behind carefully worded press releases and spokespeople who are well coached in just what and what not to say. But NetNoir, with its Black Erotica site, turned controversy into a channel to public awareness. It was an opportunity to educate us about its cause.

Mind share is not a sum, but a multiple. Each citation in the press, each recommendation by an expert, each presentation at a conference, generates a ripple effect. Get enough of this ripple effect and your projected image can far exceed your size. Make sure, though, that you are developing the products that will match all of the expectations you're creating. In the end, sizzle can open the door—but it's crucial to have some substance behind it or all that mind share can turn to rot.

Chapter 7

Dance with Your Customer

Capturing the greatest amount of mind share doesn't always result in customer acceptance. Although being identified as the market leader will attract potential customers, it won't take long for that interest to turn into criticism if you don't supply the market with a viable product. One surefire way to lose market share is to supply customers with all of the bells and whistles, but nothing else. What most customers want is something that works consistently and simply. To borrow what Gertrude Stein once said of Oakland, "There's no *there* there" in a lot of technology products. I can't count the flurry of press releases and phone calls I've received pushing a *very important breakthrough* that turns out to be only a slight improvement—like a glitzier interface or a faster connection—that scarcely matters to the user.

> "The way to get lasting mind share is by designing products that people want."
>
> —Stewart Alsop, venture capitalist, New Enterprise Associates

A good example of the problem—products that don't meet a customer need despite clouds of hype surrounding them—is the personal digital assistant (PDA). PDAs were pocket-size devices, smaller than laptops, that were supposed to revolutionize computing by becoming as ubiquitous as the pencil. You could carry around your address book, jot down notes to yourself, get faxes, even phone home with a combination PDA/smart phone. Companies big and small jumped on board. In 1993, John Sculley, then head of Apple, ignited the fire with his now widely disparaged prediction that the launch of Apple's PDA, Newton, was the start of a "trillion-dollar" business. The market research firms, though not as wide-eyed as Sculley in their projections, also produced optimistic numbers about how big the market could be.

AT&T Corporation, anticipating that traffic over its telephone network would be greatly enhanced by all these PDA connections, scooped up two start-ups—both now defunct. I remember feeling a certain amount of skepticism while watching an elaborate, well-produced AT&T video on the interconnected future, in which a bride-to-be happily shopped for her wedding dress via her handy PDA. But despite the technology industry's reputation for cold-hearted scrutiny of new ventures, it can really be duped by a hot prospect. No one wants to get left out of the next big thing. So venture capitalists poured money into fledgling software companies writing for the PDA. Microsoft chipped in with a scaled-down Windows dubbed WinPad. Apple would be reborn with the Newton. If there ever was a case where mind share, at least within the industry, preceded reality, it was the PDA.

Unfortunately for PDA champions, the first round of products flopped, notably Apple's Newton, whose hand-writing recognition feature produced error-ridden transcriptions that became a standing joke even among the nontech press. The biggest problem, though, was that consumers couldn't figure out what to do with the things. There already were cheaper, more reliable, electronic devices that kept track of addresses and phone numbers. And laptops, getting lighter all the time, satisfied the demand for portable business uses. Apple eventually refined the Newton, and it has gone on to become a useful niche product in fields like pharmaceutical sales and health care. U.S. Robotics, now part of 3Com, proved that there was a broad market for personal computing devices with its hot-selling PalmPilot, introduced in 1996. Instead of being a stand-alone device, like the original Newton, the PalmPilot is a mobile organizer that interacts with your desktop computer.

Ultimately, says Stewart Alsop, a respected technology journalist and now a venture partner with New Enterprise Associates in Menlo Park, "the way to get lasting mind share is by designing products that people want. If you have that kind of product, you have the opportunity to create mind share." Alsop has a formula for developing a successful product: Q (quality) + I (innovation) + S (smarts) + M (money) − P (pain) squared = success. The quality part of the equation: "Does it work?" The innovation part: "Does it do something that people want that they couldn't do before?" The smarts: "Does management understand the process of delivering and communicating with the customer?" And the pain: "What are you asking the customer to go through for your product to work?"

Alsop's equation revolves around the customer, who has, in today's technology world, become an active partner in developing new products. At customer-focused companies like Siebel Systems or PeopleSoft, the line between where the customer ends and the design team starts is blurred. "You go live with your customers and find out what their problems are," says executive search consultant David Powell. "Then you make something that solves their problems." Powell is also a limited partner with the venture capital firm, Sequoia Capital. He recalls one meeting where a CEO stood up and complained that customers weren't buying his products. "I said, 'Why don't you make something they want to buy?'" That company, Powell recalls, was driven by its engineers, as many start-ups are, "and they were just designing stuff when there were faster, cheaper alternatives already out there."

Of course, the tricky part is that the true breakthrough product has to leap ahead of what the customer wants into the realm of vision. Technology companies (and for that matter all companies) are constantly walking the tightrope between trying to be first to market with a new innovation and failing because their timing is off, or becoming so cautious that they're relegated to the backwaters of incremental improvements. Says Alsop: "Clearly, companies attempt to develop technologies in advance of what people want. It's partly intuitive. The value to the customer is what hasn't existed before. You can't ask customers what they don't know about." However, the technology industry, thanks to the Internet, e-mail, and other advances, is finding ways to mesh innovation with almost instantaneous customer feedback and product refinement.

■ CUSTOMERS ARE KING

As we learned in the last few chapters, Siebel Systems is completely focused on its customers—so much so that conference room doors are named after the company's major customers. The company is so adamant about customer satisfaction that employee compensation is tied to it. Each quarter, Siebel pays an outside research firm to interview customers and rate their satisfaction level with the company and its products. Variable pay for all employees is tied to how that survey turns out. Vice President of Engineering Bill Edwards says one question on the survey sums it up: "Would you buy Siebel software if you had to make this decision again?" For the last four surveys, he tells me, 100 percent of customers said yes. A related question, "Do you intend to buy future products from this company?," also got a 100 percent "yes" response rate. "We wrap our arms around the customer, and we don't let go," Edwards sums up.

At PeopleSoft, the fast-growing enterprise software vendor introduced earlier in the book, it's not easy to rile easygoing CEO Dave Duffield, unless you mess with a customer. "The only time I've ever seen him mad is when a customer gets let down," says Rick Bergquist, PeopleSoft's vice president of technology. "If you want to see Dave angry, screw with a customer. Even then, he'll want to know, what can we do to fix it?" Duffield, who personally visits with major customers, says that the Ford Motor Company bought PeopleSoft's line of financial software even though the company did not have the international presence or the product breadth of competitors SAP AG and Oracle. "They selected us because they liked and trusted us," Duffield says. "Ford viewed it as a 20-year marriage and said they were selecting a software company, not a product. We lived with Ford for six months and spent $1 million proving to them that we could offer the system they need."

The attitudes of Siebel and PeopleSoft represent a profound shift from the early days of the technology industry, when companies just threw out a product and waited to see if it caught on. In the early days of high tech, it wasn't considered essential that customers be completely satisfied. This was the case because there were few product choices; and technology solutions took so long to get up and running that customers found themselves bound to a vendor once they had installed its system. Oracle's early databases were notorious for this. In his book *The Difference Between God and Larry Ellison,* author Mike Wilson describes how Version 1 of Oracle's database was known as "the roach motel," because data went in and it didn't come out. Within the industry, it's understood that Version 3 is usually the first reliable release of a software product; the company works out the bugs in the initial two releases. It wasn't until Windows 3.1 that Microsoft really got it right and the new operating system became a big seller. This problem is not confined to software vendors. Look at the infamous flaw in Intel's Pentium chip a couple of years ago. The company waited until it was flamed on the Internet and in the press before fixing a problem it had known about for months.

But today the tide is shifting to focus primarily on customer needs. The proliferation of technology into all facets of work has made computer glitches and shutdowns more intolerable. With computers and software running their mission-critical applications, corporate specialists are becoming more sophisticated about technology, both in selecting it and in insisting that it function properly. Businesses have many tools, like the comparative reports done by the trade press and industry analysts, to help them assess new technology. On the vendor side, increasing competition gives customers more choices, and more clout. Finally, the Internet's facilitation of word-of-mouth recommendations and disparagements makes it tough to keep any problem with new products a secret; witness Intel's experience with the Pentium flaw. A sign of the shift in attitude within technology companies is that marketing is no longer viewed as a poor stepchild to engineering. The roster of high-tech CEOs, which once contained only leaders with a technical background, now numbers among its ranks people who came from a sales and marketing background, like Siebel or Autodesk's Carol Bartz.

"As each new generation of technology becomes cheaper and simpler, you get a broader, less knowledgeable audience. That's when the company must move from being engineering-driven to being marketing-driven."
—Jim Moore, founder of GeoPartners and author
of *The Death of Competition*

In another shift, as technology has evolved, so has the customer base. With the first generation of new products, you generally have very complex, customized, expensive solutions aimed at a few major customers. "As each new generation of technology becomes cheaper and simpler, that gets you a broader, less knowledgeable audience," GeoPartners consultant Jim Moore points out. "That's when the company must move from being engineering-driven to being marketing-driven," if it hasn't already done so. Engineers want to stick to the high-level complex products, Moore notes. "When a company listens to its engineers, they make faster and faster machines for smaller and smaller market subsets." Instead of confining product development to only those subsets, executives "must understand the dynamics of technology evolution, identify which customers they want to respond to, and make sure they pay attention to emerging customers."

■ TAKING A BATH ON YOUR PRODUCT

What happens when you don't pay attention to customers? A popular, albeit repulsive, saying in the technology industry refers to "drinking your own bathwater"—which happens when you're so sure your product is going to be hot that you forge ahead in spite of warnings to the contrary. The PDA fiasco was a classic example of the industry gulping down gallons of its own bathwater. Although every start-up now knows the sad tale of the PDA (and if they don't, their venture capital firm is sure to tell them about it), repeating such a mistake still happens when companies get so caught up in the excitement of what they're producing technologically that they forget to apply any real-world checks and balances.

This is what happened to OnLive of Cupertino, California, a company founded in 1994 with the goal of creating 3-D virtual-world software. Their product would allow an individual consumer, using an avatar (an on-screen persona), to maneuver within a simulated environment and interact with others who are also in the environment. It was a field with such sizzling potential that OnLive attracted $23 million in investment money from one company, Softbank, alone. Other high-profile investors included Intel, AT&T, and three of Silicon Valley's most prestigious venture capital firms.

Betsy Pace,* who brought a marketing and business development background, became CEO of OnLive in 1995. With short dark hair and minimal makeup, Pace comes off as straightforward and hard-working. She looks you squarely in the eye and doesn't try to dodge questions. She is not a technologist, she confides, and she believed the promises of OnLive's first product, which was 75 percent finished when she came on board. "In the Internet feeding frenzy, we all drank our own bathwater, thinking our customers couldn't possibly understand what they wanted," she says. "As a first-time CEO, I got caught up in that. We built what we wanted." And that was very advanced technology called "virtual worlds," which many experts were touting as the next generation of consumer business. OnLive bought into the vision as well. It was a big mistake, Pace admits now. "I didn't stop in my tracks and say, what are we fixing?" OnLive launched the product, called Traveler, in 1996 with 6,000 trial users. "We asked them what they wanted the product for and the silence was deafening. There was no compelling need."

And without a compelling need attracting customers to buy virtual-world software, there was no revenue stream from advertisers. "We had a lot of meaningless mind share," says Pace, "but no revenue." She wound up taking the company through a painful repositioning (see Chapter 10) that involved layoffs and a switch from consumer to business product development. Since 1997, OnLive has been developing products that enable real-time group communication through a combination of audio, text, and 3-D applications which can be viewed via the Internet or inter-

*In 1998, OnLive merged with two other small companies, Electric Communities and The Palace. Pace left the company, replaced by Larry Samuels.

nal corporate communications systems. Uses include on-line training, business collaboration, customer support, personal communications, and Web-based marketing. "We've shifted all of our resources out of virtual-world development into business," says Pace. "Now we're customer-driven, business-oriented. With hindsight it seems really obvious." These days, OnLive is careful to solicit feedback before—rather than after—it launches a product, allowing customers to tell the company if they can use what it's making.

➤ What Happened at Autodesk

At a time when Internet fever had reached epidemic proportions, OnLive, a young company with a new CEO, had somewhat of an excuse for its misstep. But start-ups aren't the only ones who drink their own bathwater. Autodesk, the respected 17-year-old manufacturer of software for computer-aided design (CAD) introduced earlier in the book, had a similar disastrous experience with its introduction of a new release of its lead product in late 1995. With her typical candor, Autodesk CEO Carol Bartz recalls, "Autodesk was in an arrogant phase where we didn't get enough customer input and support. You have to go through that to know what it feels like."

Adopting AutoCAD Release 13 forced Autodesk customers to make several major transitions, including upgrading hardware, adopting a new operating system (Microsoft's Windows 95), and changing their data configuration. "We should have called Release 13, Release 1," says Bartz. "We should have renamed it so that the customer knew it wasn't business as usual." Ajay Kela, Autodesk's senior director of software development, says the biggest problem with Release 13 was its poor quality and lack of customer feedback. Autodesk had worked with so many iterations of AutoCAD that it assumed it knew what its customers wanted. "We had dozens of programmers working on the release," he says. "Nobody was controlling it. All these programmers were creating components and R13 started to bloat." When the product first shipped, customers expressed their unhappiness with the slow performance, but by then it was too late to fix the overloaded program. "We went through four upgrades and the performance was still mediocre," Kela says. Autodesk results suffered, with revenues dropping from $534 million in 1996 to $497 million when the fiscal year ended January 31, 1997. Worse still, Autodesk's net income dived from $88 million in 1996 to $42 million in 1997.

Introduced in May 1997, Release 14 of AutoCAD rectified the sins of the earlier release. "We were maniacal in what this product had to be," says Bartz. Kela adds, "It had to be blindingly fast and put the productivity back. We put software into our customers' hands to measure the amount of mouse clicks it took to do a particular job. We asked what features they wanted." Autodesk shipped Release 14 to selected sites of major customers to get early feedback. Five Autodesk managers worked with the sites. "The customers could contact us 24 hours a day," he says. By the time Release 14 shipped, 16,000 users had tested it. The new release generated outstanding reviews by industry analysts, who praised its speed, stability, and robustness. Fiscal 1998 revenues rebounded to $617 million. Autodesk learned its lesson, but at a significant cost to customers and shareholders.

■ THE ITERATIVE PROCESS

To avoid the mistakes exemplified here by OnLive and Autodesk (though they're hardly alone), progressive technology companies have embraced the notion of the "iterative process." This is a series of repeated feedback loops in which an internal cross-functional team interacts with customers at just about every step of the product development cycle. For this the team turns to what are called *alpha* and *beta* customers—who agree to install and test new technology and help the vendor iron out the bugs before the product is shipped for general use. Alpha customers, who are fewer in number, get the product in a very early stage and work closely with the manufacturer to refine it, as Autodesk did with Release 14. Beta customers test a product that is almost ready for commercial release and look for unforeseen glitches. The experiences and comments of these customers are used to perfect the product in an ongoing two-way process. This can take months or even years, depending on the complexity of the product, but in today's marketplace that long a time frame is becoming more and more unacceptable. The trend is toward shorter development cycles. Toward this end some companies, particularly in the Internet content market, create their products "on the fly" and then refine them based on the customer response. But the desired balance is to minimize product development time *and* catch problems before the product is widely distributed.

"We take a position on how something should be done and test it very early with customers. It's much cheaper to change it than to throw away two and a half years of development."

—John Hart, Chief Technology Officer, 3Com

For instance, Open Market invites potential customers in for interviews and also observes customers at their own place of business to determine the requirements for its Internet commerce products. These requirements can include speed of transactions, how many transactions must be processed, and who interacts with the product. "We have a rigorous process of weighting those requirements and building products that will satisfy the need of a targeted customer," says CEO Gary Eichhorn. "Once you understand the requirements you can be innovative and creative to solve the problem." Among the questions that Open Market asks its partner/customers: "Where do you see the majority of your business coming from in five years? How do you perceive your distribution channels developing? What business are you going to be in?"

Time Warner's Pathfinder Web site was one of Open Market's early customers. "I worked personally with them on redesigning our screens and buyer flows," says Eichhorn. Another customer, online content producer CNET of San Francisco, "helped us in designing our electronic software distribution strategy." And British Telecom was a partner in figuring out how to incorporate Europe's value-added tax (VAT) systems into an international version of Open Market's electronic transaction product.

3Com Corporation's John Hart, senior vice president and chief technology officer, estimates that he spends one-third of his time with customers. "We take a position on how something should be done and test it very early with customers. It's much cheaper to change it than to throw away two and a half years of development," he says. In the early 1990s, Hart was working on a new product for adding bandwidth to a part of corporate networks called the wiring closet. He brought in two people from a major customer, who told him that the product added bandwidth in the wrong place. 3Com revised the product.

"By embracing customers and learning from them, you find new opportunities for your technology."
—Nick Grouf, CEO, Firefly Network

Firefly Network CEO Nick Grouf drew on his previous experience at McKinsey & Company in establishing customer interactive processes. Barnes & Noble, the bookstore chain, utilized Firefly technology in launching its online bookstore. Firefly's "relationship management software" lets Barnes & Noble connect customers who choose certain books online with others whose tastes are similar. The software then makes suggestions as to what additional books someone may want to buy, based on his or her own tastes. "We sent some of our best engineers to live with Barnes & Noble," says Grouf. "Not only did we learn a lot about B&N, but we learned a lot about ourselves, too—about what we need to do for our customers. By embracing customers and learning from them, you find new opportunities for your technology." Though not all customers get such specialized treatment, Firefly in general forms a cross-functional team that engages in a structured set of customer interviews, asking what the company is doing right and what it can do to improve a product.

Michael Rothschild, president and CEO of Maxager Technology, started his company as a result of experiences with a customer. In a previous life, Rothschild undertook a lengthy assignment for a division of National Semiconductor Corporation, during which he derived his idea for a new type of factory information system software. "I founded Maxager because I was thinking about the economics of the factory floor and the need for an up-to-the-minute, precise view of what's going on in the company," he says. Now two years old, Maxager is putting the finishing touches on its first products, which include a plant floor data collection system and a method for managing manufacturing inputs and outputs. "We're always making choices as to what we can afford to work on. We've made a list of 145 enhancements that would help the product, but we have to go through a triage process," says Rothschild. "It's a matter of how many balls can you keep in the air at once."

To help select from among those 145 enhancements, Maxager turns to its customers, polling them as to which advances would be more useful than others. "It's an iterative process between what our offering is, what we thought was needed, and what people are saying to us," Rothschild notes. "We get a lot of ideas from customers." One example that has now been incorporated into Maxager's product is offering a button on the touch screen called "quick look" that shows where all the pieces of work are in a designated product area. Having real customers use products like this early in the development cycle has proven to be an essential strategy for businesses in all industries.

■ FEELING THEIR PAIN

Stewart Alsop is right when he makes pain a big part of the equation for developing a successful product. Go to almost any corporate customer that has participated in an information technology overhaul and the people involved will rail about glitches, crashes, downtime, retraining personnel, and learning new processes. It's change. And change is always painful. To understand how to lessen that pain means understanding the corporate customer and its environment. That's why leading technology companies become as familiar with their customers' problems as their own. This learning process happens from the top down.

Open Market's Gary Eichhorn is a case in point. "I probably spend one-third of my time with customers," he says. "Last week I made eleven sales calls." Not only does this CEO call on new customers, he visits existing customers to ask what the company should be doing differently. Eichhorn also surfs the Web to check out customer sites, a habit he's trying to instill in the rest of the management team. According to Eichhorn, "The foundation of a great company is understanding what's going on with customers. You must go out on bad calls with dissatisfied customers. I want to be in there up to my shoulders, feeling their pain."

PeopleSoft also wants to know about its customers' pain, and it's willing to find out in a public setting. At its annual users conference, where customers, engineers, and executives interact to discuss future and present products, PeopleSoft sponsors open sessions in which customers can get up and complain about anything related to PeopleSoft products. Sarge Kennedy, who as an R&D product manager is a fixture at the conference, tells me that CEO Dave Duffield conducts the gripe sessions himself. "He gets customers together in this open forum and asks about their problems. The following year he'll get up and say, 'Here's all the problems you told us about last year and here's how we fixed them.' And he has the satisfaction ratings to prove it. I've never seen a problem that lasts more than a few months."

There's another kind of pain that a technology vendor can turn to its advantage: the pain of need. When you're trying to overcome the skepticism that greets a new product, find the leading-edge customers who have a problem—preferably in a mission-critical area—that simply can't be solved by existing technology. Technology companies seek out the first 5 percent of customers who are experiencing the pain of not having a solution so acutely that they will take a crack at an untested product. Most often, these 5 percent are in financial services, telecommunications, and aerospace—all hotly competitive, fast-changing, technology-dependent industries. Says consultant John Hagel: "The most difficult customers are in many ways the most valuable customers," because if you can solve their problems, you can presumably solve anyone's. "The really important customers are the 5 percent who are at the leading edge," he adds. "They should become partners with you in enhancing the product so that it becomes more valuable."

■ WHAT CUSTOMERS DON'T KNOW

Of course, if all you ever do is listen to customers, you run the risk of taking only incremental steps to improve your product and missing out on the breakthrough that could transform your market. Sometimes the most dangerous position in the industry is to have a large installed base of customers you have to service, making it impossible to leap boldly forward where no one has gone before. This is why IBM failed to exploit the personal computer and the microprocessor, ceding dominance to Microsoft and Intel. It's also why, with the emergence of the Internet, sassy start-ups see the opportunity to defeat much larger, richer competitors. A standing joke in the industry is: "How could God create the world in six days?" The answer: "He didn't have an installed base."

"There's a constant stream of information coming into the company from customers. However, that stream has to be processed by executives to make sure it fits together."
—Eric Benhamou, CEO, 3Com

So how do you mesh the pleas of customers to nudge the existing product toward what they want with the grandiose ideas of your technical visionaries, who would like nothing better than to cannibalize that very product in favor of something newer, faster, sleeker, and better? "If we just listened to customers it would drive the company into the ground," says Eric Benhamou, chief executive of 3Com. You have to provide the business judgment and vision that augments the customer's nearsighted view. Benhamou spends about one week each year with his company's Strategic Advisory Council, composed of chief information officers from 10 to 20 of its most important customers. Other customers participate in technical advisory councils and conferences at which 3Com engineers are also present. "There's a constant stream of information coming into the company from customers," says Benhamou. However, he adds, "that stream has to be processed by executives to make sure it fits together." One way 3Com does this is by holding a monthly meeting involving Benhamou and the executive staff, "where we brainstorm everything that's happened in the past month and paste [representations of] it on the walls. You can walk around and see what's happened. This is where market shifts are first documented. This is how patterns begin to emerge."

Andy Payne, an engineer and vice president at Open Market, says that technology companies must balance the needs of customers who want an incremental solution for an existing model with the company's desire to push the envelope. "If you let customers design your products directly, you don't end up with much innovation," he says. "You have to engage the customer in a way that cuts through what they think they want to what the problem really is." He compares this to researching the local real estate market. "Why does someone really want to sell their house? Maybe they want to go live on a golf course." Then you talk to several people selling their houses and start building a pattern. "There are a lot of people who want houses on golf courses, so maybe we go buy a golf course." Back in the technology world, you poll customers and find out what features they want, and discover overlapping patterns. "You play customers off each other. How does this compare to another problem from this customer?" Once you understand that, you can innovate a solution, he says. "Drill to the middle of the rock and innovate back out. You can innovate and still be customer-driven."

"You drag customers kicking and screaming into the next paradigm shift."

—Roger Sippl, CEO, Visigenic Software

Visigenic Software's consummate entrepreneur Roger Sippl, who likes nothing better than to be poised to take advantage of the next paradigm shift, says that customers "never ask for the next leap forward." Basically, "you drag customers kicking and screaming into the next paradigm shift with a lot of convincing." How does the paradigm shift occur then? Of course, he says, "the breakthrough

VIEW FROM THE TOP

Carol Bartz, CEO, Autodesk

On Managing in High Tech:

"High-tech executives have to deal with more ambiguity, more speed, and more 'help.' Our customers tend to be very vocal. We don't need consumer groups to regulate our industry. Our customers band together in impromptu consumer groups. You have to manage all that information. We've been using the term *virtual corporation* for five years—we've expanded the application to dealers and customers. Engineers, managers, and customers all interact on our Web site."

On Managing People:

"I'm a big believer in hiring very smart, very nice people with a sense of humor. I have a swoop style of management—let these people do their jobs and swoop in if they're not. They don't know where I'll be from minute to minute and it keeps them sharper. I hold people responsible for what they do."

On Corporate Values:

"People want to go home at night and say 'I'm proud to be working at Autodesk. I know when I make a decision that I'll be respected for that, and I have some control over my life.' We have this concept of shared responsibility."

On Innovation:

"If we move into new markets and segments, there's plenty of space to innovate. It's just as important to make sure our established products are still innovating. We have to listen

(continued)

VIEW FROM THE TOP (Continued)

---

to what our customers are asking for and stay a step ahead. With Release 13 we got two steps ahead—too far. One of the healthy debates we have is between marketing and engineering. Everybody is more interested in listening to the customer after Release 13."

On Winning Mind Share:

"In our niche we're the big guy. If you go to CAD shows we're the volume leader. Our volume is more than all of our competition combined."

On Managing for Sustained Success:

"It's about attitude—how you support the organization as a management team. I believe at any given day at Autodesk there are enough bright people. You can keep innovation and flexibility going. People have got to be able to tell you the bad and the good and feel equally comfortable. Then you wrap structure around that environment. We work with managers to make sure they understand the importance of communicating. If the channel is open, the information can flow both ways."

---

idea comes from the enterpreneurial mind who generalizes from what they're really asking for and comes back with an elegant solution. You listen to a dozen customer problems, determine what they have in common, and figure out how to solve them all at once."

PeopleSoft's Duffield has already moved his company toward the next paradigm shift. A year and a half ago, he approached Ken Morris, cofounder of PeopleSoft and its chief technology officer, and said, "It's 1987 all over again. What would you do if you didn't have any customers?" Morris took about 15 people and took on the charge of reengineering PeopleSoft's core architecture—the software code that's at the center of all its products. The new architecture "may never see the light of day," Duffield admits, "but if the world is ready to accept the changes, it will be killer architecture. We hope, in a very bizarre sense, that it will be hard to get from where we are today to this new structure." Hard in the sense that it will force PeopleSoft to cannibalize its very successful existing product line. As they say, no pain, no gain.

■ THE BOTTOM LINE

As the examples in this chapter demonstrate, high-tech companies use specific processes to help products serve their customers more effectively and engage them in product development. One process is going out to the customer and having company engineers work side-by-side with the customer's employees. "Go to a customer and build something for them," says William Metzger, president of Assets Unlimited in Campbell, California, a high-tech human resources consulting firm. "Make your product integral to whatever the customer is doing. You don't develop a product and then try to convince people they need it. You've got to make the customer's experience your own." At Intuit, a Mountain View–based manufacturer of financial and tax software for homes and small businesses, founder Scott Cook borrowed techniques he learned at consumer powerhouse Procter & Gamble to accomplish that. Intuit engineers follow customers home and watch them load the software and use it for the first time.

Technology itself can be used to simulate customer experience. Auto manufacturers are now using virtual reality software to allow designers and engineers to experience a new car's performance and the driving experience before it gets off the drawing board. Visualization can be used with services as well as products. Andersen Consulting's Joe Carter provides multimedia demonstrations to executives on how a new business process will work. "I see a business process playing out and visualize how people will do their work. We script out mini-plays so executives can see what's going on. If I've got them sitting on the edge of their seats, I know we've got it." Architects and developers use virtual reality to show how the space within a new office or home will flow.

Early adopter customers, though they may not represent the broader base you want to reach eventually, are crucial to product development, especially in burgeoning markets. "You go into the marketplace repeatedly with small, low-risk experiments that allow you to learn quickly what the customer wants," says author Gary Hamel. "It's expeditionary marketing, which Apple and the Newton failed to do. The customer set in that early period is not necessarily the customers who buy it. Within that early product vision you're no more than 30 percent right. You get the other 70 percent by learning as rapidly as possible where the real mother lode of demand is and who your partners are."

Another tactic is to recruit people into the company from your targeted customer base, which was the strategy Tom Siebel and his namesake software company adopted. "If you decide there's a need to be the Office Depot or Staples of the Internet, the people who win will be former general managers from Office Depot or Staples," says venture capitalist Robert Reid. "People who come from the center of the space you're going after are the ones who have the intimacy with the market." He notes that Jeff Bezos, the CEO of online bookstore Amazon.com, "surrounded himself with talent from the bookstore industry" before launching the Internet-based service.

Never forget, though, that customers can relay the problems they want solved, but they cannot tell you how to solve them. They can communicate to you what their business is today, but not what it may be in 20 years. "There's still the leap-of-faith phenomenon," says venture capitalist

Jim Breyer. "For the very newest technologies you can't do focus groups to validate it. Management teams have to trust their gut." Ultimately, you need to strike a balance between technological vision and the commercial viability of the project.

Geoffrey Moore, the marketing consultant, points out that building new technology is an art, not a science. "Technology creates solutions before the problem is known," he says. "You start with a sense of aesthetics— technology offers a more friction-free, faster way to do something. You're building something that's an act of beauty." Even if the product initially fails, it may be gloriously reborn, as the PDA was in the PalmPilot.

Chapter 8

Brainpower, Inc.

The most important asset a technology company has is brainpower, which resides in its people. The technology industry depends on a constant stream of new ideas and innovations that come only from people. Its explosive growth, propelled by the need to keep pace with competitors' innovations and the development of new markets, requires the constant infusion of smart, talented, creative people, not just in product development, but also in marketing, sales, management, and support. This hunger for good people drives a lot of the high-tech management activities already described in this book. Cultivating people is the top priority of high tech's most successful companies, which go to great lengths to make the workplace challenging and compelling; to accommodate employees' needs and lifestyles; to reward achievement; and to not penalize honest mistakes.

The best technology companies understand the value of their employees and use teams to make optimal use of their brainpower. High-tech start-ups are built upon a cadre of talented people with ideas—the evangelist/leader (see Chapter 2), a technical visionary, a small group of engineers, and one or two marketing and finance experts. Then you march this group through what industry insiders call "the Valley of Death," the initial phase of a start-up, when imminent demise looms but which provides the baptism of fire that melds the disparate individuals into a team. According to Yankee Group Consultant Howard Anderson, "Going through the Valley of Death does give people a cause to rally around. There's no place to hide in a start-up. There's a great spirit of camaraderie, but you have to pull your weight."

For a growing company, the real challenge of retaining employees comes after it emerges from the Valley of Death. By then, members of that hand-picked team have time to take a deep breath, wipe the sweat off their brow, look around and ask themselves, "Is this really what I want to be doing right now?" For a lot of talented people, the answer, all too soon, is "no," because another start-up, promising a new adrenaline fix, beckons. Annual turnover at an average high-tech company in Silicon Valley is on the order of 20 percent. So, for a technology company, continually renewing the challenge and encouraging the esprit de corps is an absolute condition of survival. High-tech headhunters judge the health of a company (or rather, the lack of it) by the number of resumes they get from its employees. "Apple burned out one of my fax machines," complained one headhunter late in 1997, because so many resumes from disaffected employees were pouring into his office.

Many high-tech companies enter a kind of limbo at some point after their founding, usually after the first product has been launched. They're doing well, they've got customers, they're tinkering with follow-on products, but that early spurt of raw excitement has ebbed. Waiting to cash in the stock options when the company goes public is one potent lure countering the drop in excitement. Those who come on board before the IPO are eligible for attractive options that can make the holder an overnight millionaire or multimillionaire once the IPO occurs. Even after the IPO, stock options remain a vital part of high-tech compensation. A survey by iQuantic, a San Francisco–based consulting firm specializing in high-tech compensation, reported that 100 percent of technology executives, 85 percent of managers, and 42 percent of other employees participated in stock option plans in 1997. But now that all companies are offering stock options, they aren't quite as effective in attracting and retaining employees as they used to be.

"Paying [employees], treating them with respect—those are necessary but not sufficient. You have to make them feel like they're making history."

—Jim Moore, founder, GeoPartners

If money is no longer the key motivating factor for keeping talented people, what is? It returns to the intangibles, satisfying the higher needs of self-esteem and self-actualization that psychologist Abraham Maslow identified in the 1970s. "You have to give people a sense of being part of an unparalleled opportunity," says GeoPartners' founder Jim Moore. "Paying them, treating them with respect—those are necessary but not sufficient. You have to make them feel like they're making history." In the 1980s, Apple under Steve Jobs did that very well: Employees felt they could change the world with the Macintosh computers they were designing and building. The company "was very successful at creating a culture that attracted the type of people they wanted," says Stephen Combs, managing partner of the executive search firm Juntunen Combs Poirier in San Francisco. In early 1998, Apple's turnaround was starting to rekindle that feeling.

■ THE CIRCLE OF GROWTH

Technology companies that enter what consultant Geoffrey Moore calls "the tornado," where annual revenue growth of 100 or 200 percent is not uncommon, have a corresponding need to hire people at nearly the same rate. Barbara Beck, Cisco's vice president of human resources, joined the company in 1989 when it had fewer than 200 employees. Today there are over 11,000. Cisco's revenue exploded from $69 million in 1990 (it wasn't public in 1989 and did not release revenues) to more than $6 billion in 1997. The intuitive assumption is that you add people, you grow. But actually the relationship is the inverse of that. In technology, you can't stay static in products and revenue and expect to attract good people. "Stability equals death in this industry," says consultant John Hagel. "The more growth you can drive as an enterprise, the more opportunity you create for talented individuals." It's a rather vicious circle: A company that has exciting prospects, like Microsoft, attracts more of the people who can create more growth and more excitement. The company that's struggling, like Sybase, loses the very essence of its future.

Any company that expects to recruit and retain talented people will have to change for them and with them. Andersen Consulting's Joe Carter suggests that technology companies ought to do what amounts to a start-up every 18 months, by introducing a new product cycle that feels like an entrepreneurial venture. "Get the people who want to be innovative behind that," he suggests. "Put them in charge of the new products."

It's not just change, but change coupled with some sense of underlying continuity. Even as you create new opportunities, you need to offer employees a sense of continuity and cohesiveness. It's no longer a military, command-and-control pattern where you just point people in the right direction and say, "charge." Instead, you must build a compelling case for why your company exists and have your employees buy into that. A major attraction to professionals working in high tech is the opportunity to create the next Microsoft. "People like to know that they're changing the world, that customers love them because of that," says Igor Sill, a 14-year executive search veteran and managing partner with Geneva Group International in San Francisco.

"With this kind of motivation they're not going to leave for an extra million or two in stock options. People have a great fear of leaving something that's great."

■ PROCLAIMING THE MISSION

One company that's done a good job of imparting a sense of larger mission in its employees is NetNoir, the African-American Internet content provider introduced in Chapter 6. CEO and founder E. David Ellington, a lawyer by training, is clear about his goals: He's building a company, not a mecca for black employees. "I have investors who expect me to run this as a business," he stresses. "I tell people that they're not thinking this through when they say the first thing I should be doing is training all the black people in how to do this. I'm the president of a company and I have to make payroll." Ellington is smart enough to know that even though he'd like to see so many African-American companies on the Internet that ethnicity is no longer important, right now his visibility is enhanced by his company's outright ethnic orientation. From the beginning, he set out to create the sense of making history that Jim Moore talked about. Ellington deliberately launched NetNoir on June 19, 1995, an important date in black history, because it commemorates the day in 1863 when slaves first heard about President Lincoln's Emancipation Proclamation. NetNoir's target audience is educated, middle-class, self-aware blacks—of whom an estimated one to five million are online. "We want to present our culture and our content in top-shelf fashion and address the needs of our community," says Ellington.

It is a compelling vision for people like Joseph Mouzon, vice president of sales and marketing, who joined NetNoir from the much larger Working Assets Long Distance, where he was director of business services. "For the first time in my career I'm able to combine the experience of being an

African-American and helping my profession," he says. "I don't have to explain or decode anything. I feel value here in every single experience I've had as a black American."

Cofounder and chief technology officer Malcolm Cas-Selle echoes that commitment. "It's different than someone just looking for a job. I'm willing to risk everything and put in as much time as is necessary because this is my company," he says. NetNoir is not the most financially successful company on the Web, nor is it the most generous in its employee compensation, but it does have a cause that binds people together.

In hiring, NetNoir tries to recruit a cross section of people interested in this cause—creating exciting content for an African-American audience. A majority of the company's employees are black, but one-third are not. Ellington runs an open office, with no dress code and no set hours. What compels people to work is a sense of shared mission, not directives. "We have a very loose environment with empowered employees—just go and do it," he says. "I want people to be responsible and appreciate it." Though NetNoir's environment lacks structure, it works because the company hires responsible adults who share the organization's vision.

■ LITTLE HOUSE IN THE VALLEY

Some technology companies will bend over backwards to keep their core talent—the engineers who write the code and design the products—from defecting. From the heart of Silicon Valley comes one strange-but-true tale of appeasing a star engineer. Ipsilon Networks* of Sunnyvale, founded in 1994, competes in the crowded networking

---

*In December 1997, Ipsilon was acquired by Finnish telecommunications company Nokia.

field dominated by Cisco by marrying two technologies (Internet protocol or IP and asynchronous transfer mode or ATM) that many experts considered incompatible. Consequently, attracting and retaining brilliant engineers is essential. "What we do is identify people we consider the stars and give them good salaries and the right amount of stock," says Brian NeSmith, Ipsilon's boyish-looking president and CEO. "They're people we bet major chunks of the company on." But sometimes, that's not enough.

Ipsilon had one engineer, Greg Minshall, who, in common with everyone else, sat in a cubicle in the middle of a "cube farm," as industry wits have taken to calling the expanses of gray cubicles. But noise-averse Minshall longed for an office, or at least someplace quiet to write his code. Finally, after months of pleading by the engineer, NeSmith decided to act. One weekend he recruited several friends, including an architect, and they built a small yellow house around Minshall's cubicle. The edifice, only ten feet tall and about sixty-four feet square, has a real door with a doorbell that works, a shingle roof, lighting, and even siding. Minshall came to work the following Monday in early 1997 and was dumbfounded. "I was totally blown away by it," he told me via e-mail. "When I walked in, my jaw dropped almost to the floor, and it took me at least that full day to recover." The house "made me feel incredibly special, and I like it quite a bit," he says.

Engineers are the creative engine of Silicon Valley, notes Ipsilon founder and chief technology officer Tom Lyon, who is an engineer himself. "They're also the weirdest people you can imagine," he adds. When NeSmith refers to his engineers, he sounds like a fond father describing high achieving but troublesome children: "They're babies, they're sensitive, they need attention. They get petulant, vindictive. But they have remarkable spurts of brilliance and insight." Ipsilon has a "playroom" with beanbag chairs and a Ping-Pong table (slated to be replaced with a pool table) to amuse the children when they're not working. Ipsilon remains engineering-driven, says NeSmith, with other parts of the company "sitting in support of that intellectual capital."

Like a parent, NeSmith knows he has to maintain some semblance of control and set some limits. He characterizes his management style as informal and egalitarian, but not wimpy. The informality was in evidence in his apparel: shorts and a bright green T-shirt, which nicely set off his shock of red hair. "I very seldom give orders," the CEO says. "I like to arrive at a rough consensus. If someone feels really strongly about something and has the facts to back it up, then that will carry the day." On the other hand, "I'm not a touchy-feely kind of nurturing guy. If people are not performing, harsh decisions are made."

Here's one: In the early days of Ipsilon, "we were having problems with the sales force," recalls NeSmith. Sales weren't ramping up as expected, and "there was an argument as to whether it was the products or the sales team." The company undertook some product improvements, but not much changed. After a number of hallway discussions and meetings, "I made the decision—we fired the entire sales force (eight people) and changed the organizational structure." NeSmith says Ipsilon had the wrong people for the kind of product it was selling. The original sales manager wanted a bureaucratic organization with probationary periods for new hires, and other formal structures. "You can't live with this sort of environment at a start-up," NeSmith says. Lyon supports the CEO's drastic action: "It was very clear something was wrong and that something had to be done about it."

Although opportunities abound for innovative people who can deal with the often-chaotic, demanding working conditions of a high-tech company, it's not to everyone's liking. At Ipsilon people either sink or swim. "That's intentional," says NeSmith. "I'm not a hand-holding type of manager. It's my job to correct or avoid the wrong decisions. There are times I see people doing something where they're making mistakes but they're learning from that. The whole key is trying to differentiate between mistakes and serious problems." The cover-your-ass mentality prevalent in traditional, bureaucratic companies has little credence in high tech. There's just no time for caution. The market's demands are changing so rapidly and new competitors are emerging so often that it's better to act quickly, even if you're not making exactly the right move, than to wait.

"What we've done from very early on is communicate responsibility for each person's respective part of the undertaking. We wanted empowerment to be more than lip service."

—Pat Nettles, CEO and President, Ciena Corporation

■ STAYING POWER

Far from Silicon Valley, Ciena Corporation, located in Linthicum, Maryland, demonstrates that even relatively conservative companies can adopt techniques that empower and uplift employees. Ciena, founded in 1994, went public barely three years later and leapt to a healthy market cap of more than $5 billion with an advanced technology called dense wavelength multiplexing. What was so exciting about this tongue-twisting technology was that it dramatically boosted bandwidth capacity. Like a side road that is expanded into a highway, the greater the bandwidth, the more network connections your computer can make. If the Internet ever crashes (some pundits say that it's just a matter of *when*), limited bandwidth will be the culprit. Ciena's technology boosts the capacity of fiberoptic cable in telecommunications networks so that more data can be transmitted at faster speeds.

Even after its initial public offering made Ciena's employees extremely wealthy, all but two of the original twenty people remained with the company, which has now ballooned to more than 800 employees. CEO and president Pat Nettles, employee number two, is the true exemplar of managing the white spaces in between what everyone else does. "I like to think I'm dealing with people who are better at what they do than I am," says the stolid 54-year-old CEO. "I don't try to drive them to do something. What we've done from very early on is communicate responsibility for each person's respective part of the undertaking. We wanted empowerment to be more than lip service." Nettles deliberately looks for people who are willing to take the lead in making decisions about their area. "There's an adage that you hire people for what they know and fire them for who they are," he says. "I try to hire people for who they are and fire them for what they don't know."

"Intellectual opportunity, autonomy, and creativity—those are the cutting edge."
—Rebecca Seidman, Vice President of Human Resources,
Ciena Corporation

Empowerment carries beyond the professional level of engineers and sales managers. Rebecca Seidman, vice president of human resources development, recalls that when the company moved into large-scale manufacturing, "we bought into the model that says when you get to a certain size, you need a supervisory level." So Ciena dutifully interviewed and hired three supervisors for manufacturing. "Within two weeks the people on our assembly line walked into my office and said, 'Why do we need supervisors? We were doing fine without them.' " The employees proposed that whatever the supervisors were doing, they could handle. "They were right," says Seidman. "We fired all three of the supervisors." Even at 800 employees, the company hasn't installed any manufacturing supervisors. Instead, the sales department informs the manufacturing teams how much product Ciena will have to deliver to customers each month. The team reconfigures the assembly lines to meet the demand, including determining how many hours of overtime will be needed and what the scheduling will be.

Seidman, who was previously a marketing and administrative principal at an accounting firm, views her function at Ciena as building the framework of people needed for success. "We believe we have the top people in the industry and we want to keep them," she says. "Money and stock options are a satisfier. With annual performance reviews, we will make changes to meet the market if it's needed." Ciena, like other high-tech companies in a competitive labor market, must keep pace with rising salaries and benefits offered by others. Again, though, employee satisfaction goes beyond money. "Intellectual opportunity, autonomy, and creativity—those are the cutting edge," says Seidman.

Ciena is careful to recruit people who fit into the company ethic of work hard, play hard. "For every position, even an entry-level assembler, we do two days of screening before that person comes on board," Seidman says. "If they get through the two days, there's a very high probability that person will fit in here." Once people are aboard, "if they love their work, my job is to identify the barriers keeping them from doing it and create a more flexible environment that encourages them to stay," she says. Seidman works with the top 20 percent of achievers to develop each employee's "personal dream plan" that the company does its best to fulfill, including paying for training and development courses, restructuring work hours, and providing family support. It all adds up to the kind of environment that people don't want to leave.

■ A MILLION-DOLLAR MBA

It's not only the engineers who find opportunities for personal achievement and financial prosperity at high-tech companies. Revisiting Siebel Systems, introduced in Chapter 5, we find a prime example of a company that has enriched many early employees, both financially and otherwise. Take Heather Beach, the 29-year-old director of operations. An economics major, she joined in 1993 when Siebel consisted of five people and CEO Tom Siebel sat at a folding table in the middle of a decrepit office in East Palo Alto. "I came as the office manager," Beach recalls. She'd had several marketing jobs, but wanted something more. "I took a pay cut to come here; it was a risk. But I thought, 20 years down the road, what will I regret more, a pay cut, or not having taken the risk and missing out on this opportunity?"

The decision paid off. "I was able to participate in stock on a basis normally not offered to my position." Beach couldn't afford to take all stock and zero salary, an option offered to all employees, but took as much stock as she could. "The payoff right now is about fifty times what I started with. It wasn't until a reporter called me that I realized I was a millionaire on paper." But more than that, Beach feels like she's had the equivalent of an MBA at Siebel. In late 1997, she had just overseen the development of Siebel's sparkling new facilities. "When we started, this building was a concrete slab. In two and a half months, we were able to move in. I manage all the facilities and corporate real estate."

Like everybody else at Siebel, Beach has helped out with making the company's sales software products work.

She comes in on weekends to help with the "bug blitzes," in which employees use the software themselves to find out what the problems are. "We all help iron out the bugs," she says. "Even if the financial equity position hadn't happened, I've learned a tremendous amount."

CEO Siebel says Beach is one of about 80 millionaires in the company—representing almost one-third of the workforce. Traditional companies are starting to offer stock options on a limited basis, but Siebel Systems' employees own roughly 70 percent of the company, which had a market valuation of nearly $2.5 billion in mid-1998. Perhaps that accounts for their dedication to Tom Siebel, who has a reputation for being one of the toughest CEOs in Silicon Valley. People work nights and weekends; take red-eye flights whenever possible; and conform to Siebel's unusually strict dress code (at least for the technology industry), which specifies formal business wear even on Fridays, the traditional "casual day" in corporate America. "There's a level of intensity here that I haven't seen at other companies," says Chris Stauber, director of product marketing and a 15-year veteran of the technology industry. That intensity is enforced by a rigorous hiring process. "An average candidate will meet a dozen Siebel people, any one of whom can veto someone from getting hired," Stauber says.

In addition, there are no pampered cliques or special treatment. "We try to foster this notion that we're all in the same boat," says Bill Edwards, the company's vice president of engineering. Engineers are treated as adults who can do what they're supposed to do. "In some organizations what engineers do is create a structure with T-shirts and beer busts to try to foster behavior that meets business needs. We feel that it's much more satisfying for engineers to understand customer expectations." At Siebel, engineers "get motivated knowing they're making the business successful," Edwards notes. What makes engineers and other employees like Beach want to stay? Most of them don't need the money anymore, but Siebel has given them the chance to create something great.

■ HIGH TECH'S PYRAMID

Returning to the basic strategy of rewarding employees through compensation programs, the high-tech industry has a compensation pyramid where the three major layers are stock options, base pay, and incentives. Stock options are still the basic foundation, the get-rich-quick draw for young engineers graduating from Stanford University or MIT. Technology companies use options about three times as aggressively as general industry, according to Mark Edwards, president of iQuantic, the compensation consulting firm. (See charts in Appendix C.) IQuantic arrived at this by calculating the stock option "burn rate"—the number of options granted in a year divided by total shares outstanding—which is 3.5 to 4 percent in publicly traded technology companies, versus only 1 to 1.5 percent in nontech industry. Another difference Edwards has found in his research: Stock options in high tech are granted to a much broader swath of employees than in nontech industry, where they are usually confined to the executive level.

"Stock options send a message that you're trying to get by on energy and bright ideas and dreams of making it. The magic is we're all going to share in the wealth."

—Mark Edwards, President, iQuantic

"Stock options are increasingly an accepted coin of the realm in high tech," Edwards says. "If you don't do stock options, you won't get off the ground." More than just the monetary value, the options "send a message that you're trying to get by on energy and bright ideas and dreams of making it. The magic is we're all going to share in the wealth." And on a practical basis, options comprise the most cost- and tax-effective way to compensate someone, particularly for a start-up.

However, there's an increasing disparity between the options that incoming employees expect and what companies can afford to give. "Technology employees are becoming more sophisticated as they sell, or lease, themselves to potential employers," Edwards says. A few years ago, employees would accept the number of shares initially offered; now they're pushing back and asking for more. Meanwhile, the investment community that funds technology companies, composed of venture capitalists and institutional investors, is becoming more proactive in keeping an eye on how many options are being granted. He adds that before going public, "it's not uncommon to see 20 to 30 percent of the stock in the hands of employees, although that's so variable it's hard to pin down." After the initial public offering, companies have to replenish their option pool by buying back stock, a move that must be approved by shareholders. "A lot of institutional investors automatically vote no if a company asks for more than five percent of the outstanding shares for option grants," Edwards notes.

The next piece of the compensation pyramid is base pay, although this is declining in importance, particularly at upper levels. In 1997, iQuantic's high-tech compensation survey showed that only 25 percent of CEOs' pay came in base salary; 17 percent was incentive or variable pay; and 58 percent was in stock options. For chief financial officers, the comparable figures were 31 percent in base pay, 14 percent in variable pay, and 55 percent in options. Even for individual employees, base pay as a percent of total compensation was dropping. A quality assurance engineer got 72 percent of compensation in base pay in 1997, compared to 82 percent in 1992. Options and variable pay jumped from 18 percent in 1992 to 28 percent five years later. (See Appendix C.)

David R. Mather, a managing director with the national executive search firm Christian & Timbers, points out that a decade ago technology start-ups had a very different compensation structure from mature companies.

"A start-up used to be able to say, 'Come to work for $45,000, but we'll give you a lot of options,'" he says. "Today the competitive environment is such that start-ups have to be just about as competitive in salaries, because the bigger companies will also throw in a lot of options. The reward systems are moving closer together." He suggests that high-growth companies, which are going to need to recruit a lot of people, should study their competitors' compensation packages and position themselves in the middle. You don't want to be too much above competitors' compensation, because then people think there's something wrong with your company—or too low, because the best people won't consider you.

■ THE BOTTOM LINE

The high-tech industry's egalitarian treatment of employees is permeating nontechnology companies as well. Spurred in part by criticism of the chasm between the compensation granted to top executives versus ordinary employees, corporations are turning to stock options as one way to close that gap. At the 200 largest U.S. companies, options represented 11.8 percent of all outstanding shares in 1996, compared with just 6.9 percent of shares in 1989, according to a survey cited in the September 21, 1997 *New York Times*. The same article estimated the total value of shares set aside for options at all U.S. public companies at a stunning $600 billion, 10 times the $60 billion set aside in 1985.

"Companies will have to think through what is the best way to allocate options and other compensation to get the most value," according to iQuantic's Edwards. The attraction of variable pay, such as profit-sharing plans, is that it shares both the risks and rewards. "When times are bad, all employees tighten their belts; when times are good, everyone gets a piece," he says. But, like other experts, he cautions that options and compensation aren't enough. "You

EXPERT OPINION

Howard Anderson, founder and president of the Yankee Group and founder of Battery Ventures, both in Boston

On the Differences between a Start-up and an Established High-tech Company:

"First is the influence of the venture capitalists, who would rather have a high-risk company with potential for a high level of success than low risk. A typical high-tech company is often risk averse, but the VC is high reward, high risk.

Second is good management styles. The high-tech, fast-growing company will skip on management process in an effort to increase speed, decrease costs. There's no training, no history of pulling people along or promoting from within. You grab from wherever you can get talent.

Third is lack of predictability. Plans gyrate wildly from week to week. There's no cash cow product to finance new development. Everything is new development. The companies are in a loss mode in their early days. There's a sense of Brownian motion."

On the Motivation of the High-tech Industry:

"The desire to build elegant products and solutions. In high tech the issue is less personal wealth accumulation and more the desire to make significant products or services in an ever-changing market. In high tech, there's a higher scale you'll be judged on. Can you find that innovative product that serves a real need? Can you continue to build innovation into this product? Find new distribution channels?"

On Succeeding:

"The single most important thing for a high-tech company is to pick the right segment. If you miss the segment

(continued)

EXPERT OPINION (Continued)

slightly but are well run you may have another shot. If you pick the right segment and don't execute you'll be okay. If you pick the wrong segment you're doomed."

On Sustaining Growth:

"You want to get through the Valley of Death as quickly as possible to building the first product and shipping it."

On the Future of Your Start-up:

"Your true enemy may be your investment banker. When do you keep growing versus when do you sell out? If you've got a real hot company in the right market and you can go for the gold, a big IPO, selling too soon may be the wrong way to go. An IPO with a class underwriter is the gold. If you're dealing with a secondary underwriter you're not going to get coverage. There are advantages to selling out: Get liquidity, personally and for your investors. Free management to do what they do best."

have to have the money stuff there, but you also have to create the right culture, give people steep learning curves, a holistic environment, and attractive employment opportunities."

It's not only in compensation where the concept of employee ownership is being reflected. The technology industry has provided both the tools and the methods for allowing employees to share more fully in information flowing through the corporation. For instance, many companies utilize internal corporate networks (intranets) to let employees view and modify their own records, relating to personal leave, vacation, benefits and the like, without going through personnel departments. Corporate mission statements, press releases, Securities and Exchange Commission filings, and other documents are posted on Web sites available to employees as well as the general public.

Even old-line industries such as auto and steel manufacturing are coming around to utilizing employee teams who, to a large extent, govern their own work. Driven by overseas competition and the impact of technology, unions and management are cooperating to an unprecedented extent to make the workforce more productive.

In sharp contrast to the nineteenth-century Dickens-like image of the workplace as a site of miserable, back-breaking toil, the words "challenging" and "fulfilling" predominate today in many positions. With U.S. unemployment rates near historic lows, the field of competition is shifting from products to people, and the fast-growth technology industry is leading the way in offering exciting opportunities. People "have to be happy in their jobs," says three-time entrepreneur Roger Sippl, CEO of Visigenic Software, Inc. But they're not happy just sitting around with nothing to shoot for. They want real goals and measurements of when they achieve those goals. "Letting people do whatever they want isn't what keeps them. It's giving them the chance to apply their skills and win," he says. "Becoming rich isn't the driving force. If I'm a brilliant engineer, I'm going to prove that brilliance when I join a start-up and use my skills to make it succeed."

If you remade that prototypical Jimmy Stewart movie *It's a Wonderful Life* and set it inside a company making leading-edge technology, every employee would fancy himself or herself as the star. Because all of them can look back and say, as a result of being here, "I made a difference in the world." That, at least, is the dream.

Chapter

Mergers and Alliances: Picking the Right Partner

Selecting the right partners and developing the most beneficial cooperative structure has become as essential to sustaining profitability in the high-tech arena as having innovative products or mind share. In the best tech companies, these three elements are inexorably intertwined. When you choose to gain mind share by establishing a standard, you need to have the agreement and support of other companies in your market. To expand your market reach, you may need to use someone else's distribution channel or sales force (as Check Point did early on in enlisting Sun Microsystems to sell its firewall). Going global or investing in additional research and development initiatives often involves the support of corporate colleagues and competitors. Some of the biggest investors in entrepreneurial technology companies are not venture capitalists but large technology companies like Intel, Microsoft, and Cisco. They take equity positions in smaller entities whose technology may complement their own. In turn, the small companies reap the benefits of added funding as well as association with a star.

Alliances in the technology industry can take many forms. Howard Anderson of the Yankee Group separates alliances into four categories. At the bottom of the list is an alliance that sounds good on paper, but is meaningful only for its name value to one of the participants. Innumerable start-ups, for example, trumpet the fact that a huge and dominant player like Microsoft or IBM or HP is using their technology in some fashion. The second type of alliance is a comarketing agreement, typically taking the form of a larger company agreeing to market a smaller company's product as an add-on to its own. A variation of that, the third type of alliance, is an original equipment manufacturer (OEM) contract, in which one company sells another company's product under the first company's name. The fourth type of alliance, potentially the most valuable but difficult to pull off, is where two companies spend significant engineering time designing a product together for a single customer or set of customers.

An alliance can also be the prelude to a full-blown merger. Companies want to get to know each other before they rush into each other's arms in a permanent relationship that, if it fails, can lead to a painful separation. The technology industry's track record for successful mergers has been pretty dismal. In one of the largest merger attempts, AT&T never succeeded in integrating computer maker NCR Corporation and wound up spinning it out again. The two companies had differing business purposes and customer approaches that could not be easily meshed. Many pre-1990 technology-industry mergers involved a traditionally structured company seeking to absorb an entrepreneurial one. This stifled the innovation and creativity the larger company was initially seeking and is exactly what happened when IBM took over Rolm Corporation in 1984.

Today, however, several industry trends make high-tech mergers more likely to succeed:

➤ The first trend is intense competition and the rapid speed of innovation, which means that not even the largest, most richly endowed company can keep up with every sector of the market. So the acquisition of small start-ups with innovative technology can replace or augment internal product development.

➤ The second is the emergence of large technology companies that are themselves products of the entrepreneurial cauldron of the 1980s and 1990s, and thus more cognizant of how to avoid a negative situation when seeking an acquisition.

➤ The third trend is the tremendous increase in market capitalization enjoyed by leading high-tech companies; this enables them to use their stock as acquisition currency.

In the past, arguably the most successful high-tech merger model was that of Computer Associates International of Islandia, New York, which bought troubled companies at fire-sale prices and then stripped them down to their valuable components, like development teams and products, dumping everything else. The downside of this model was that no company would willingly be acquired by such a perceived corporate ravager, and Computer Associates was blocked from most friendly mergers. A kinder, gentler takeover model has since emerged, where the acquirer operates the new company as a wholly owned, semi-independent subsidiary, as Hewlett-Packard intends with VeriFone.

Another model, championed by networking leader Cisco Systems, involves buying small start-ups that are barely more than product development teams and folding them within the larger company's lines of business. The product team and most of the company's management are retained to add value to the bigger entity. So pervasive has this model become that some entrepreneurs now start companies with the express intent of being acquired by Cisco or one of its competitors.

Companies large and small, established and entrepreneurial, wrestle with the complexities of when to ally, when to buy, and when to continue flying solo. Like a good marriage, making a high-tech alliance or merger work depends on each partner getting value and giving it, and feeling enlarged as a result. "You have to make other people rich in a value chain that makes you rich," sums up marketing consultant Geoffrey Moore.

■ FRIENDS, PARTNERS, AND COMPETITORS

Technology products must work together to be useful—hardware with software, an operating system with an Internet browser, a computer with a router. The industry has consequently evolved into a complex web of interrelationships in which any two companies compete for business on one day and cooperate in some sort of alliance on the next. Says venture capitalist Ann Winblad: "It's like playing the game of Risk. The goal is to take over the world, and for that you have to have friends. You have to co-opt some partners to get rid of some other people from the board."

CrossWorlds Software, the start-up I've been following, has enlisted several powerful allies in its quest to link customer-oriented and enterprise management software via its processware. To make this idea work, CrossWorlds needed to partner with software companies on both sides of the divide, in addition to hardware companies and consultants. As is typical of the technology industry, some of its partners, like SAP AG and PeopleSoft, are themselves bitter competitors. Technology companies must be very nimble in choosing their alliance partners, so as not to get crushed between giants like, say, Microsoft and Sun Microsystems. CrossWorlds CEO Katrina Garnett speaks for a lot of companies who find themselves uneasily watching the titans battle. "As a company we try to be Switzerland," she says. "Our neutrality is our greatest asset."

Another method is to find a single ally whose clout is so great that you don't have to spread yourself out among numerous partners. NetNoir found in America Online (AOL) an equity partner and distribution channel. CEO David Ellington was at first reluctant because he wanted to handle distribution himself. "I had been practicing law in the entertainment business, and one of the biggest life lessons I learned was that black people never control distribution," he says. But AOL, which allowed NetNoir to control its content area, "turned out to be a perfect fit." Besides giving NetNoir access to the largest online audience in the world, AOL invested $1 million in the fledgling company, enabling it to expand to the Internet. NetNoir gave its partner some value as well, says Ellington: "We've created $1 million in positive publicity for AOL."

"One of the hardest challenges in high tech is to decide when is the right time to begin considering alliances, who's the right partner, and what's the right deal. You have to get all three of those right."
—Jim Breyer, venture capitalist, Accel Partners

Starwave Corporation, another Internet content provider, has two heavy-duty sugar daddies in Paul Allen, the wealthy cofounder of Microsoft, and the Walt Disney Company,* which reportedly poured $100 million into the private company in 1997. Based in Bellevue, Washington, Starwave, which provides sports, news, and entertainment sites, had already been a partner of Disney subsidiary ESPN in producing ESPNET SportZone on the Web. Since the Disney investment, Starwave has added a site devoted to online content from another Disney subsidiary, ABC News. "Disney is a very careful and process-oriented company. They weren't so sure they wanted a partner," says Starwave CEO Mike Slade. It was the potential for exploit-

---

*In May 1998, Disney exercised its option to buy out Allen's remaining stake in Starwave.

ing ABC's broadcast content in the electronic world that got Disney on board. The deal is structured so that Starwave employees, along with Allen and Disney, own the company. There's still a possibility of taking Starwave public if Disney wants to recoup its investment. "The other option is, this business is the *Titanic* [the boat, not the movie], and they write us off," he acknowledges.

Managing alliances in the technology industry requires the delicacy of a diplomat. "One of the hardest challenges in high tech is to decide when is the right time to begin considering alliances, who's the right partner, and what's the right deal," notes venture capitalist Jim Breyer. "You have to get all three of those right. You have to develop a sense of when to do the deal, when to start talking about it. You have to narrow down the group of partners and figure out organizationally who's a champion, who needs to make it work personally." At the same time, a company does not want to compromise its own independence in an alliance. For most companies, the best strategy seems to be hedging their bets by undertaking multiple alliances and then going through a winnowing process as they determine what works and what doesn't.

■ RETHINKING MERGERS

Until several years ago, every start-up tried to remain independent and eventually become a public company through an initial public offering. "Only if they failed at that would they be sold, usually at a fire-sale valuation that made everyone unhappy," remarks investment banker Chip Vetter. "Then Cisco started acquiring companies at better than public market valuations. The stigma of not going public was removed." The reasons for the change in attitude were twofold: First, Cisco and other acquirers were admired and emulated by the companies they bought, removing some of the sting of a takeover. And second, the acquirers were paying prices that were often above what the company might have gotten in an IPO.

This latest merger trend originated with the networking sector, as different technologies converged and customers sought total solutions rather than pieces of a puzzle. To match the speed at which the market was developing, networking companies began buying all the different pieces—technologies like routing, remote access, and switching—that they couldn't develop fast enough internally. Cisco is credited with pioneering the strategy, but it soon was mirrored by its competitors, among them 3Com and Ascend Communications. One of Vetter's client companies was sold to 3Com for $170 million. "Now, it's respectable to be sold," the investment banker says. Larger companies are focusing on marketing, branding, and customer relationships and are, in effect, outsourcing much of their research and development to smaller companies they then acquire.

"If things are moving fast and you can do anything to make them move faster, it makes it more difficult for the competition to maintain the pace," says venture capitalist Don Valentine, founder of Sequoia Capital. As Cisco became the dominant networking company, its distribution channels became so powerful that "acquisition had an incredibly high revenue impact," Valentine says. The acquired company's products suddenly had the added value of Cisco's clout with customers, and sales jumped. Most of Cisco's acquisitions were tiny companies concerned primarily with product development, enabling it to quickly leverage its distribution channels to accommodate the new technology. However, each of the networking leaders, including Cisco, has done at least one big deal.

■ THE CISCO KIDS

In the past few years, Cisco has acquired some two dozen companies, typically in stock swaps, and made minority equity investments in another 15. Since Cisco became a public company in 1990, its stock has increased more than a hundredfold in value, giving it ample resources to undertake acquisitions. Says chairman and former CEO John Morgridge: "We're in a very unforgiving environment that presumes that not only do you have good vision, but you're always right." Through mergers, someone else can be right some of the time. "We do not choose to be insular and cling to one technology. When a customer said to us, we're thinking about buying one of these whatsits, we often bought the company that did the whatsits," he explains, with characteristic wit.

Michelangelo "Mike" Volpe, vice president of business development, recalls that Cisco made its first acquisition in 1993, when it bought Crescendo Communications for $89 million. The product line that Crescendo brought is now doing about $1 billion in annual sales. "That acquisition went incredibly well," says Volpe, "so well we decided to do a few more." The accompanying business strategy, which grew out of the acquisitions, was to become "an end-to-end solutions provider in a market growing rapidly in volume and technology."

Cisco's preference is to buy small companies, geographically close, that can be integrated swiftly into existing business units. Barbara Beck, Cisco's vice president of human resources, singles out the key considerations when contemplating a purchase as: (1) the company's management philosophy, (2) the strength of the management team, and (3) the ability of the company to fit into Cisco's culture. "It's got to be a culture mind meld," she says. Cisco puts together an acquisition team that includes representatives from human resources, finance, business development, engineering, and legal. "We've never had an unfriendly takeover," Beck adds. "We do acquisitions for the people, not so much the product. The only way it works is if the people want to come." Again, we see a trend toward knowledge management and the importance of brainpower. Generally, an acquired company's engineering and marketing groups are integrated into an existing line of business, with the management team staying on to head product development and marketing. Sales groups are combined within Cisco's sales force.

Adds Volpe: "The management team is one of the key assets. The hardest talent to find today is senior management." He estimates that about 50 percent of the chief executives and 75 percent of the senior management at acquired companies have remained with Cisco, a contrast both to the fire-sale approach of Computer Associates and the often-hostile takeovers in the nontech world. "As an entrepreneur you can start a company or try to run something excellent and unique within a larger entity," Volpe says. "At Cisco you can be the best in the industry." He compares Cisco's strategy to buying a seed and throwing soil around it. "We look for the Cisco kids—companies that would look like us in five to six years." What Cisco emphatically doesn't want is a fire sale. "We don't troll the bottom of the barrel. We attempt to accelerate momentum that already exists."

Krish Ramakrishnan, director of engineering for Cisco's Internet Appliances Business Unit, can attest to that. He came on board in October 1995, when Cisco bought Internet Junction, which he had cofounded. "We were down the street from Cisco, privately funded, and two years old. To say we were extremely happy [with the acquisition] is an understatement. Cisco was a recognized leader in networking." Ramakrishnan and his cofounders realized that networking was a market where "we needed a big corporate player behind us to make our product successful." He adds, "What technologists like to see is the success of their product. We jumped on the Cisco bandwagon because it was great for our product."

No one from Internet Junction had left Cisco as of late 1997. Ramakrishnan oversees a group of 20 people who continue to make "entrepreneurial decisions" about their product. Cisco acts like a venture capitalist in deciding which projects to fund; then the product team carries it forward. "What the Cisco culture boils down to is common sense," he says. "It's all about what's right for your product, and people respect that. We haven't experienced any culture shock. We feel like we've been here since the founding of Cisco."

■ STRADDLING STRATACOM

While most of Cisco's deals have followed the "Cisco Kids" strategy just described, the company has engaged in one big deal, with mixed results. In 1996 Cisco bought StrataCom in a $4 billion stock swap. At the time, Cisco had about $4 billion in annual revenue and employed 8,200 people, while StrataCom was a $332 million company with 1,200 employees. StrataCom, located near Cisco in Silicon Valley, made high-speed data-transmission products that Cisco wanted in order to broaden its product line. StrataCom's products were used primarily in the telecommunications industry, but Cisco saw an opportunity to incorporate the technology into other types of networks, especially as it strove to integrate audio and video with data.

"StrataCom was a good experience because we gained insight on the unique challenges of doing a big deal versus a small one," says Morgridge. "We felt we had gotten pretty good with the small deals. Whenever you feel like that you better watch out." He admits StrataCom took a lot longer to assimilate than expected, particularly getting its sales force up to speed on Cisco's products, and vice versa. StrataCom was so big that Cisco created a new business unit to encompass it. "We did a great job in integrating manufacturing, services, purchasing, but we weren't very successful in integrating their sales force," Morgridge says. Salespeople "have a zero-sum-game mentality" that makes them reluctant to sell new, unfamiliar products.

Though Morgridge does not rule out another large acquisition, it seems unlikely. Says Volpe: "There's a strong preference toward sticking with a model that works. StrataCom was an exception. It was a fast-growth local company, but it takes a tremendous amount of management bandwidth to handle an acquisition that size. We don't have to spend as much bandwidth on smaller acquisitions. And we get a better return on investment on small deals than big deals." Cisco continues to tinker with the acquisition process. "As long as we can continue to buy great small companies at a reasonable price, we will," Volpe says.

■ MERGER STRATEGY: THE MORE, THE MERRIER

3Com, a major Cisco competitor, is also bingeing on acquisitions. "Part of our strategy is to roll enough balls down the hill to keep up with demand for new technology," says John Hart, senior vice president and chief technology officer. "A few years ago we saw a way to do that with start-ups—let other companies roll the ball and then take them over." But all the competition for start-ups has boosted the price of acquisition, so 3Com is becoming more selective. Generally, says Hart, 3Com tries to make its own internal incremental improvements to existing products, and to acquire companies when it needs to get into new areas. For example, 3Com wanted to move into a portion of the networking market called *hubs,* which do with data what airlines do with flights at their hubs. "We acquired a division of another company for $20 million, and now we're doing $1 billion worth of business from hubs," says Hart.

To gain the necessary bulk to compete with Cisco, 3Com decided that small acquisitions alone would not be adequate for it to achieve parity. In June 1997 it bought U.S. Robotics (USR) Corporation in an $8.5 billion stock swap, one of the largest mergers in the history of the technology industry. As mentioned previously, USR makes the hot-selling PalmPilot, but what 3Com really wanted was USR's modem technology so that it could enhance its ability to offer remote access to corporate customers. The combination of 3Com, based in Santa Clara, and USR, based in Skokie, Illinois, created a global giant with $5.5 billion in revenues and 14,000 employees in 45 countries.

The move was not universally applauded, however, since so-called mergers of equals—companies of similar size—had a rocky history in the technology industry. Says Cisco's Morgridge: "USR will be an interesting test for 3Com because it's so big." With Cisco's acquisition of StrataCom, "we managed to do a reasonable job, but they were located right down the block." When I pressed 3Com CEO Eric Benhamou about the wisdom of such a risky deal, he confessed that buying USR "weighed a lot on my mind." But Benhamou believed that 3Com had learned enough from studying its own mistakes and those made by others "that we could successfully pull off a transaction of this magnitude."

In considering the USR acquisition, at the direction of their methodical CEO, 3Com's executives made a list of all the mistakes they had observed in other companies undertaking major mergers and checked off each as one "that we weren't going to make," Benhamou says. The first error to be avoided was doing a transaction just to add size without a clear strategy. "We had a strong strategic reason why we had to do this and why it created a tangible benefit for customers," says Benhamou. 3Com was concentrated in the local-area network (LAN) market, while USR's expertise was in wide-area networks (WANs). LANs operate within limited geographical boundaries, such as a corporate headquarters or a university, while WANs reach out to encompass remote users and consumers across vast areas. In addition, 3Com and USR had almost no overlap between their respective product lines, which meant that a merger would not involve massive layoffs and cancelled projects. "You didn't have to kill anything in order to start building on the merger," says Benhamou. With USR, 3Com is pursuing four markets: the corporate enterprise, Internet service providers, small businesses, and consumers. In addition, USR makes 3Com nearly equivalent to Cisco in revenue, and "we're much bigger in terms of the number of users we have connected to our networks," notes Benhamou.

Since the merger, 3Com has reorganized the combined company into three business units, each with its own sales organization. The first unit, called client access, is part USR and part 3Com. The second unit, aimed at telecommunications and Internet providers, is mostly USR, and the third, the corporate enterprise, is mostly 3Com. "Both management teams agreed we needed to make it one company very quickly," says Debra Engel, 3Com's senior vice president of corporate services. "We announced all the new compensation and benefits within two weeks of the merger being completed. We thought it better to make a few mistakes and fix them as we go rather than wait." A steering committee with management from both companies created a document dealing with core values and how the combined company would be governed. The three business units had two months after the merger in which to come up with the same thing. That sent a message that the new management team, which included USR's Casey Cowell as vice chairman, wasn't going to tolerate delays in getting everyone and everything to work together.

Any merger of this magnitude consumes large amounts of management time and effort, which can be a serious distraction in a sector as competitive as 3Com's. On the other hand, such a merger offers not only the usual economies of scale, added bulk, and greater recognition, but subtler benefits such as new management talent. Indeed, 3Com's savior, Benhamou himself, came from an acquired company, Bridge Communications. "It's too soon to tell on USR," says venture capitalist Michael Moritz, whose firm was an early investor in both 3Com and Cisco. "You won't know until about five years from now whether this merger was successful."

■ CASCADING BENEFITS

Shortly after 3Com completed its merger with USR, Ascend Communications, a smaller but fast-growing competitor of 3Com and Cisco, took over Cascade Communications Corporation in another bicoastal merger. In a crossover typical of the industry, Cisco had an equity investment in Cascade, a Westford, Massachusetts–based manufacturer of networking equipment used by telecommunications carriers and Internet service providers. Cisco makes such equity investments with an eye toward a possible merger, but Cascade's rich share price and its East Coast location were deal killers for the market leader. "Cascade was very pricey," says Cisco's Morgridge. "Just because you have equity doesn't mean you're going to buy. Our vision of where they're going and where we're going have to match. There has to be a long-term and short-term payoff for both sides. Geography was also an issue."

But in a market where competitors increasingly need critical mass to offer the services and broad-based product line their customers demand, Cascade proved compelling enough for the Alameda, California–based Ascend (previously introduced in Chapter 5) to plunk down $3.7 billion in stock. "You have to increase your mass, either by internal growth or acquisition," says Ascend CEO Mory Ejabat. "You do a small acquisition to gain the technology. You do a larger acquisition to gain distribution channels and mass." He disagrees with Cisco's emphasis on geographical closeness. In the networking business, "you've got to be able to remotely communicate. If you can't do that effectively you should get out of that business," he says bluntly, with an underdog's feistiness. "Before we acquire a company we make sure we have good synergy." He and Cascade CEO Dan Smith talked for at least two years about doing a deal. "We have the same vision."

Cascade is now one of four business units inside Ascend, and it's still run by former CEO Smith, now executive vice president and general manager of the Core Switching Systems unit. Each business unit is responsible for its own engineering, product marketing, and manufacturing. The salespeople are integrated within Ascend. "Before we ever signed the merger agreement, we knew what the new management team would look like, which salesperson would have what account," says Bernie Schneider, Ascend's vice president of strategic business development. The merger required the elimination of 250 positions out of a total of about 2,000. Let go were engineers, salespeople, and marketing people across both companies. "You can't have one organization taking all the hits," Schneider says. "If you give people good packages, you can minimize anxiety by moving as quickly as possible, so we did the layoffs all in one day. The people who stay feel like the ones who left were treated with respect."

The Cascade business unit will continue to operate out of Massachusetts. "Being physically separate means they can stay focused on their products," says Jeanette Symons, cofounder of Ascend and chief technology officer. "What we bought was a great company with a great product and great engineering team. We've got a bigger bag of toy makers so we can build more toys." In contrast to Morgridge, she believes big mergers can be easier than small ones, "because you're forced to focus and make decisions," while "with the little ones nobody pays as much attention."

Ascend, which is still dwarfed by Cisco and 3Com, is now in a position where it could buy more companies—or get swallowed up itself. "Are we an acquirer or acquiree? We're agnostic," says Schneider. "We want to bring the best products to our customers. We're for whatever would allow us to do that." That comment epitomizes the current sea change in the technology industry. Paced by the fast-growing networking sector, the industry has now accepted, and even embraced, friendly mergers as a prelude to improved products and greater clout.

■ THE HP WAY: NOT!

Some mergers don't involve assimilation. Although Hewlett-Packard's "HP Way" has reached the status of near-religion in the technology industry, the company it recently acquired for $1.3 billion in stock, VeriFone, doesn't plan to be a convert. "I've no idea what HP's management style is and no interest in it," says VeriFone CEO Hatim Tyabji. "We will not be immersed in the giant. HP wants us to bring our culture. We're a separate, independent legal entity. So long as we perform, they'll leave us alone." Sounding a bit like Star Trek's Federation of Planets resisting the Borg, he adds, "There's no question of assimilation. We won't be assimilated. We're a bunch of street fighters."

The HP-VeriFone merger is one of those working experiments that pervade the technology industry. HP has done mergers in the past, notably of Apollo Computer, in which it completely absorbed the acquired company. But Apollo was struggling, while VeriFone is healthy and fast-growing. HP wants an entree into the electronic payments world, which VeriFone can provide. VeriFone wants the service and customer support capability that HP can provide, to handle its emerging consumer business. "For me to build those from ground zero would be very difficult and time-consuming," says Tyabji. "HP gives us an instantaneous and well respected presence globally." HP also brings deep pockets, notes Roger Bertman, vice president of corporate development for VeriFone. "They have lower costs of capital, great consumer channels and procurement capabilities," he says. "It was clear as we were moving into electronic commerce that a half-billion-dollar company couldn't fund all this itself. We needed the clout of a bigger player."

Even a reigning giant of the technology industry like HP needs to be shaken up occasionally, which VeriFone and its virtual organization intend to do. "We bring a sense of urgency, disdain for bureaucracy, and speed of decision-making," says Tyabji. Richard "Rick" Belluzzo,* executive vice president of HP, agrees: "We have gotten younger in mind and spirit in working with VeriFone and seeing how fast-moving organizations can respond." VeriFone's decen-

---

*In 1998, Belluzzo left HP to become CEO of Silicon Graphics.

tralized, geographically dispersed structure is something HP wants to study. "We think that we can learn a lot from VeriFone about what it means to be a virtual company," he says. That kind of model "is the future we're headed toward, with the Internet tying everything together."

Belluzzo, who championed the VeriFone deal inside HP, worked closely with Tyabji in structuring the relationship. "If we just buy them and don't do anything with them, it's kind of stupid," Belluzzo says. "We're not going to focus on having the same payroll system or badges; we're focusing on delivering to the market." For example, HP has already assumed VeriFone's customer support service on a seven-day-per-week, 24-hour basis. Any changes to Veri-Fone "will not be so much in their internal culture as in the external products and services we deliver together. We do intend to provide them with a lot of independence but find areas where we can work together to offer customers solutions. From the front [customer perspective] we'll look seamless, but at the back end we'll be different," he says.

> "In a new market, you do alliances because you want to learn from others and coevolve with them."
> —Jim Moore, founder of GeoPartners and author of
> *The Death of Competition*

HP has proven in the past that it has the ability to reinvent itself without destroying its culture. For instance, it entered new lines of business with printers and desktop computers, and quickly moved to the top or near the top of those fields. With VeriFone and Tyabji, HP is taking on the challenge of handling what will obviously be a very opinionated, independent-minded subsidiary without damaging either VeriFone's culture or its own. Fortunately, the two companies start with considerable overlap. "Elements of our companies are similar: a high level of trust, autonomy, and respect for the individual," says VeriFone's Bertman. "Hatim is going to run this the way he always has, only now he's answering to HP rather than Wall Street."

■ THE BOTTOM LINE

When considering a merger or alliance, the smart companies look for something beyond name recognition and momentary mind share; they look for strategic value that can be enhanced by the right partner. "You have to have strategic partners, but understand the consequences of choosing one over the other," says venture capitalist Ann Winblad. She cautions that deals usually produce a champ and a chump. You want to make sure you're the champ. Adds fellow venture capitalist Tim Draper, managing director of Draper Fisher Associates in Redwood City, "Before you pick a partner you've got to figure out who needs you more, what you can do for the other company, and what they can do for you. Together you build a better service or product. You don't just ally yourself with Microsoft for no apparent reason."

GeoPartners' Jim Moore, an expert in analyzing alliances, sees the reasons for them varying, based on the stage of a market. In a new market, "you do alliances because you want to learn from others and coevolve with them," he says. As the market sorts itself out, "then you want to be a member of the preferred coalition, so you choose as powerful an ally as you can." In an even later stage, niche players start entering the market and alliances become a means of asserting dominance and blocking potential competition. Above all, a company seeks partners because it wants to concentrate on areas in which it can be an innovation leader and outsource other areas.

Millennia ago, Socrates voiced the truism that holds for any company contemplating a merger or alliance: "Know thyself." You need to understand your culture, your core values, your product line, and above all, your weaknesses.

Just how much can your management team handle? If you ally yourself with this major player, who will you alienate? Do you have enough confidence in your ability to hold your own against a larger, more powerful ally? What is your prospective partner looking for from you? Can you give it without compromising your independence? These questions become even more critical with the permanence of a merger. Maybe you should live together, in an alliance or joint venture, before you sign that marriage license. A bad merger is as painful as a bad marriage, and as difficult to dissolve.

The technology industry has proven that mergers can be accomplished with the same speed that rules other aspects of this new strategic framework. Consolidation is occurring in other fast-changing industries as well, like telecommunications, financial services, health care, and insurance. With agreeable management and a rich share price to lubricate the action, deals can be broached and consummated quickly. You do your planning up front, announce any layoffs as soon as possible, and rely on electronic communication to bridge global distances. There is no need for the acquired company to be geographically close; technology will provide the necessary communication. Hostile takeovers will remain rare in the technology industry, and probably become less frequent in other industries as well. Knowledge capital—which resides in people—is growing in importance everywhere, and people can bail out if they don't like a potential takeover.

As of late 1998, four of my subject companies—Visigenic, Scopus Technology, Ipsilon Networks, and Firefly—had all agreed to be acquired by other technology companies. In addition, Starwave had become a subsidiary of Disney, while OnLive, though retaining its name, had merged with two other small companies and revamped its management. "There's a recognition that you don't necessarily grow your own innovation," says John Carosella, Ipsilon's vice president of marketing and business development. To enter the next frontier, companies big and small enlist some help.

These deals exemplify the unrelenting competitive pressures that have caused a bunch of highly individualistic companies to embrace mergers and alliances. Even as start-ups spring to life daily, consolidation, especially in sectors where innovation and customer demands are outpacing any single company's ability to keep up, has become a fact of life in the evolution of the technology industry.

Chapter 10

The Party's Over

From the preceding chapters, it may sound like the technology industry has known nothing but good times, and indeed, it has been an industry singularly blessed by unprecedented growth rates and exploding demand. I've never seen as much wealth as I observe among these high-tech companies, where Gen-Xers are set for life with their millions of dollars' worth of stock and can afford to endow $2 million chairs at Stanford. In Silicon Valley residential enclaves like Woodside, where three acres is the minimum size for a lot, IPO millionaires plunk down $5 million or $10 million in cash to buy a home. Popular accoutrements include a full-scale gym, guest house, pool house, barn for the horse, and a minikitchen in the master bedroom. Looking at all those performance cars weaving and dodging down the overcrowded freeway, I can see why the local BMW and Porsche dealers are probably the next-richest guys in the Valley. Besides cars, the toys high-tech execs buy for themselves include fighter jets, yachts, and horses.

But technology has generated more than just individual wealth. The industry has become the engine driving much of the U.S. economy and, by extension, the world's economy as well. Approaching $1 trillion in annual revenues, information technology is now the single biggest manufacturing industry in the United States, surpassing construction, food products, and automobiles. However, because of the fast pace of change and the early cannibalization of once-dominant products, the technology industry is also one of the most volatile sectors in the United States. During the market tremors of late 1998, disappointing earnings by leading technology companies, bellwether Intel's forecast of lower demand for its chips, and the government's lawsuit against Microsoft were all cited as factors in the downturn. When the markets surged upward again, tech stocks led the way, paced by Microsoft, which joined an elite list when its market cap surpassed $300 billion for the first time. The only other company on that list is longtime blue chip General Electric.

The stock market is but a reflection (that is often exaggerated) of underlying realities. The truth is that the technology industry has produced more failures than successes, at least by the industry's own definition of success—which is for a company to acquire enough critical mass to go public or, as mentioned in the last chapter, to be acquired by a major player. The number of start-ups that achieve these goals is less than 50 percent. According to statistics compiled by VentureOne Corporation, a San Francisco firm that tracks venture capital investments, of 2,540 venture-backed companies started between 1987 and 1991, 732 went public and 411 were bought. That leaves 1,397, or 55 percent, which either are staying alive as small private companies or have bitten the dust. (VentureOne doesn't track companies that close their doors.)

Even public companies aren't immune to failure. Take the minicomputer manufacturers—like Digital Equipment Corporation, Prime Computer, and Wang Laboratories—that were once on the cutting edge of technology. During the 1970s, minicomputers—sleeker, smaller, more flexible machines than the massive mainframes that had initially dominated corporate computing—were hugely successful, and their innovative manufacturers were the Microsofts and Intels of their day. Then came the paradigm shift to desktop computers that left these companies struggling to survive, eclipsed by PC manufacturers such as Compaq Computer Corporation and Dell Computer Corporation. Most of the minicomputer companies, like Prime, Wang, and Apollo Computer, filed for bankruptcy or disappeared. The most prominent company, Digital, worked for years to fashion a turnaround, but in the end had to sell itself to Compaq. The next generation had its failures, too. For example, Silicon Graphics, once renowned for its high-powered computers used to create mind-boggling special effects in movies such as *Jurassic Park,* lost favor with the mainstream corporate market and, in early 1998, brought in a new CEO to attempt a turnaround.

Watching what a technology company does in the rough times is one of the best indicators of how it will perform in the future. After all, almost anyone can steer the ship when it's in calm waters with nary a storm in sight. Take Cisco, which has enjoyed almost cloudless skies since its 1984 founding, serving a networking market that took off with no end in sight. "This company has been fortunate," acknowledges chairman John Morgridge. "The vast majority of the decisions we've made, irrespective of the reasons or even the intellect, have turned out all right." Cisco has had a few hiccups in digesting some of its numerous acquisitions, but so far has suffered no serious downturn. Competitor 3Com, by contrast, has been through a baptism of fire with a makeover that saved the company. "If you compare our past with Cisco, we've had bad times and emerged the stronger as a result of having to change," proclaims 3Com CEO Eric Benhamou.

From start-ups that must reposition themselves because their market has failed to materialize, to mature companies whose strategies have failed, this chapter looks at the techniques involved in rising anew in an industry in which old competitors are relentless and new competitors are breeding daily.

■ RETHINKING THE PACE

OnLive, introduced earlier in this book, started out to provide consumer-oriented virtual worlds via the Internet, and when that market did not pan out, turned to developing communications software products for the business world. CEO Betsy Pace had to lay off more than a third of her workforce in June 1997 as part of the retrenchment. A first-time chief executive, Pace prides herself on being a good people person, nurturing but direct. So eliminating 30 people from a workforce of 75 was not a pleasant experience. "I was the one dragging my feet," says Pace. "My management team convinced me, you've got to face it." Before the rumors started, she called everyone together and told them that the company was facing substantial layoffs and communicated what those layoffs were as quickly as possible.

It took Pace and her management team about a month and a half to redesign the company and figure out who would go and who would stay. Then it was time to start telling people their fate. "I was scared to death," says Pace. In a small company, she was close to nearly everyone. One of those she had to terminate was a senior marketing/communications manager who was a personal friend. "I told her three to four weeks in advance that we would have to streamline our marketing organization as we shifted from consumer to business," recalls Pace. "She took it very personally, but I knew I could count on her confidence." Another person laid off was the senior human resources person, the same one who convinced Pace that the company was overstaffed for what it was now trying to accomplish. "It was readily apparent that we had too many people. Doing nothing about this would not have been supportable."

Pace drew some of her inspiration for managing through the difficulties by recalling the turbulent times at Apple Computer, where she spent eight years as a director and midlevel manager in the late 1980s and early 1990s. She left Apple in part because of the frustrations of being part of a large company that was becoming chaotic. "In the tough days at Apple the hardest thing for me was feeling impotent," she says. "Here at least we're in charge of our destiny. We can't prevent market risks, but I'm intolerant of victimization and blaming failure on something else. We succeed or fail here. This company took a turn in the road when it concluded it wouldn't become an online service but could succeed as a software developer."

Pace now believes that OnLive is stronger for having gone through the layoffs. "It was like having a heart attack," she says. "We cared a lot about the people who left. The overarching message was that we had to do this for the business. We made a generous severance. Now we're very focused and know where we're going and, for those who are left, it's a huge relief."

Ruth Hennigar, the vice president of product development, adds that some of the engineers left voluntarily because they wanted to stay focused on the consumer market. "We laid off the people who had been doing the 3-D design and graphical application, and cut back on testing people, but we didn't lay off any developers," she says. The product development team now numbers about 25, including contractors, down from 35. "Ninety-seven percent of the people believed in the new focus and the decisions we made. They were bummed when their friends left, but they knew we were making business choices that had to be made. It is brutally focusing, but it's sometimes what you need."

Like many technology start-ups, OnLive made the mistake of putting too much on its plate. "When you have too many things you could do, you try and do them," Hennigar says. The repositioning of the company and layoffs accomplished a necessary reprioritization of the company's goals. "The people I've hired since the change really see the new opportunity—the less glitzy, more practical side of our technology," she says. Hennigar is confident the company now has the right focus, though she concedes not everyone agrees. "You do what you can to address concerns, but there's a point at which you say to people, get on the bus or take another bus."

■ THE INTERNET EQUALS UNCERTAINTY

Repositioning is the rule rather than the exception for most Internet companies. The emergence of the Internet as a key resource for both businesses and consumers is such a recent phenomenon that start-ups created to exploit it often misfire. The Internet and associated corporate intranets (internal nets) and extranets (external nets that reach out to customers, vendors, and others outside the company) promise to revolutionize the way companies do business, but first the products and, more important, the organizational structures have to be developed that support the transition. The Internet enables almost instantaneous communication, information access, commerce, and entertainment, but it is also clunky, difficult to use, fraught with glitches, and stubbornly resistant to profit-making. The Internet's "for free" attitude means that companies have to give away product to establish a presence, as Yahoo! did with its search engine, then hope to capture revenue via advertising and transactions. It doesn't always work that way, as OnLive found out. Yahoo! and the other Internet companies in this book, like Open Market and Starwave Corporation, have altered their courses, too.

During Open Market's early days, from 1994 to 1996, the company was doing custom programming and running an Internet mall called Open Marketplace. But it became obvious that the way to make money on the chaotic, cutthroat Internet was to sell a product to other vendors who wanted to be there, and not necessarily be there yourself. "It was clear that our technology would be more valuable licensed out to other companies," says CEO Gary Eichhorn. "We still believed Internet commerce was going to be a major opportunity." So instead of operating an Internet mall, Open Market decided to provide others with the tools they would need to open their electronic stores. It's a common story in any new arena, from the California Gold Rush to electronic commerce: With rare exceptions, those who make the real money are not the ones who are panning for gold but the ones who sell them the picks and shovels and bread and salt. On the Internet, that means software products that allow you to process a sale or locate information or interact with a site. In mid-1996, Open Market, building on what it had learned in developing its own mall, began selling a framework for processing electronic commerce transactions, with enabling products called Transact and SecureLink.

"For the innovators and early adopters we've seen some proof that Internet commerce is real," says Eichhorn. "The amount of time it's going to take for everyone else to catch on is the question. Every new technology since the VCR has shown an exponential decrease in time of adoption." He says the decision to set up an Internet commerce site is now expanding beyond early adopters to mainstream companies, where these systems are being discussed at the board of directors level. Companies moving to Internet commerce include information providers, such as publishers of medical, legal, or financial data; business-to-business catalogs, selling products like computers, replacement parts, and office supplies; and retailers, such as Disney's online stores. To reach those segments, Open Market either acquired or partnered with companies who had the needed expertise.

Yahoo! underwent a somewhat similar experience in relation to a joint venture with the credit-card company Visa International. In 1996, when the joint venture was announced, Yahoo! and Visa intended to create an online section devoted to electronic commerce on Yahoo!'s Web site, which would sell both products and services. The two partners would share in revenue generated from the undertaking. Yahoo! CEO Tim Koogle eventually realized that was the wrong model. Rather than creating a single site devoted to electronic commerce, it was better to scatter commerce potential throughout all the sites that offered information about products or services. "There's an amazing amount of value in threading commerce wherever you can," says Koogle. "There's a contextual relationship between people getting information and making a decision about what they want to buy. You need to have both in the same place." In mid-1997 Yahoo! dissolved the joint venture, at a cost of $21 million in stock paid to Visa. The companies agreed instead to establish an Internet-based shopping guide to help consumers choose products and services they want to buy online. Koogle says Yahoo! controls the commerce side of the shopping guide, while Visa handles marketing and distribution. In addition, the two companies will collaborate on a Yahoo!-branded Visa card for use on the Web.

Starwave, founded in 1993 by the deep-pocketed investor and Microsoft cofounder Paul Allen, had enough money to go through three different business models before finding itself. The company's first incarnation was to develop content for satellite TV. Then it switched to multimedia, making CD-ROM products that featured such stars as Peter Gabriel and Clint Eastwood. Patrick Naughton, now president and chief technology officer, realized when he came aboard in 1994 that the future was in the Internet, not stand-alone CD-ROMs. In fact, Naughton only agreed to join the company after Starwave agreed to change its business model. "My objective was to bail out of these CD-ROM contracts asap," he says. "I said everything we do from now on has to be on the Internet." Today Starwave, now owned by Disney, offers sports, show business, and news sites on the Internet.

"Starwave started another incarnation after Disney [which first invested and then bought the company]," says Naughton. "We were a publishing company with a technology base. Now we're more like a software company that produces content for two very big partners," Disney and its ABC subsidiary. All the churning took its toll. "We had a lot of turnover while we were trying to figure out who we were," says Barbara Thompson, vice president of human resources. "We tried hard not to lay people off. If a project got cancelled or changed, we tried to move them to a new product, but that wasn't always as successful as we'd hoped. Sometimes people just didn't fit."

Starwave CEO Mike Slade says having Paul Allen as the company's primary backer (until Disney came along) gave it the luxury of being able to try out different business models in a wildly uncertain market. "You could afford to do things in the right way and build your own products from scratch," he says. "In the Internet everyone who's relied on third parties has gotten screwed and everyone who has built their own has been happy." On the other hand, "the disadvantage of having deep pockets is you end up putting more food on your plate than you can eat. It's like going to a buffet. Most of our mistakes have been trying to do too many things at once," he says, echoing OnLive's Hennigar.

■ WALKING AWAY FROM THE TRAIN WRECK

Internet start-ups are not the only companies that find themselves with the wrong business model. After 3Com was founded in 1979, it became a leader in network adapter cards, which enable personal computers to run networking software that allows them to share information. 3Com wanted to expand beyond that product, but was unsure whether to move into software or hardware. It tried to do both, buying Bridge Communications in 1987 for its networking software and at the same time expanding further into the hardware business by manufacturing network server computers.

That dual strategy backfired, and Eric Benhamou, a cofounder of Bridge, stepped in to pick up the pieces. "We had strayed away from the original reason for buying Bridge," says Benhamou, which was to reduce dependence on computer components. "We were below critical mass as a computer company and we were losing our edge in networking as a software company. We had to figure out what the company was about."

In 1990 he made the crucial decision to reposition the company in networking software, which at the time was a collection of disparate products such as routers, hubs, and switches, each made by a different vendor. Meanwhile, Cisco had surpassed 3Com by concentrating on what was then the dominant part of the networking market—routers. Benhamou eliminated 3Com's computer business, though he kept the cash-generating adapter cards and refocused on software. Doing so meant laying off 12 percent of the company in 1991. Since then, 3Com has gained enough market share to overtake other rivals and become Cisco's primary competitor.

At the beginning of the decade, "3Com was a train wreck," says venture capitalist Don Valentine. "They made a clever acquisition with Bridge but proceeded to ignore the people and the direction that Bridge should have taken them. Benhamou then took the company in the direction he knew was right." Adds Valentine's partner Michael Moritz: "There have been two 3Coms. The one that was going out of business in 1990, that had entirely missed a market, which is where Cisco entered stealthily from stage left and elbowed 3Com out of the way. The new 3Com is now getting back into a business that they missed."

Benhamou says 3Com went after a market where Cisco didn't dominate—smaller, non–Fortune 500 companies that were seeking one-stop shopping for their networking needs. "The strategy we used was a global data networking strategy, based on viewing networks as a system instead of individual parts," he says. "You think very differently if you own an automobile versus simply building the carburetor or the tires." He moved 3Com from a components to a system orientation and, though 3Com currently lags behind Cisco overall, its competitor's lead is diminishing. "Cisco doesn't have as much of a lead in other areas as in routers," notes Benhamou. "People who buy networks today are the midsize and small companies. To be able to reach all of these, you need a very strong brand, strong distribution channel, and broad range of products."

Barbara Shapiro, vice president of corporate communications and a 3Com employee since 1986, says the repositioning was a painful necessity. "We had to do layoffs and find ways for some of our customers to migrate to other suppliers. But Eric knew what we had to do. He understood where our strength was." Benhamou was also willing to put himself on the front line, attending numerous sessions with the financial industry and the press to explain just what 3Com was doing by emphasizing global data networking. "He was a very patient evangelist," she says.

■ TRISKAIDEKAPHOBIA (I.E., FEAR OF THE NUMBER 13) REBORN

As described in Chapter 7, Release 13 of Autodesk's lead product, AutoCAD, was disastrous for the company. In failing to get enough customer input during development and releasing the product late and riddled with problems, Autodesk saw both revenues and earnings contract in its fiscal year ended January 31, 1997. Triskaidekaphobia—fear of the number 13—was rampant among customers and within the company, where employees worried about job security and their future. In Autodesk's 1997 annual report, CEO Carol Bartz was extraordinarily frank in her letter to shareholders: "To say FY97 was a difficult period for

Autodesk and its partners would be an understatement," she wrote, and then proceeded to describe how a slowdown in Europe and the problems with Release 13 had affected the company. In a telephone survey, "our customers told us that the initial negative perception some users had of AutoCAD Release 13 during its first year on the market discouraged others. In fact . . . almost 30 percent of poll respondents had never even seen a Release 13 demo."

Besides enlisting significant customer testing and feedback for the next AutoCAD upgrade, Release 14, Bartz and her management team had many spirited debates in which they grappled with what steps to take internally during the transition. "During difficult financial periods, companies often show their true character," she wrote in the annual report. "In their rush to protect the bottom line for the short term, some companies lose sight of long-term strategies—an unwise move, in my opinion." Bartz remained true to two of Autodesk's core strategies: focusing on long-term growth, and being candid with employees, shareholders, and customers.

"We have a style here that is almost too open," says Bartz. She asks, though, "How credible are you going to be when you're pretending that something bad isn't happening? I would rather admit it and have the opportunity to explain our side of the story." Although up-and-down cycles are natural in the technology industry, the press and the competition "don't want to let go when you're in a downturn," she says. "You know you're going to come out of it. What you don't know is how deep is the trough and how long is the cycle." With the Release 13 debacle, Autodesk tried to avoid accelerating the downturn. To that end, it continued to make acquisitions to enter new growth markets, such as its consumer product line Picture This Home! The first entry in this line, using a slimmed-down version of AutoCAD, enables consumers to design a new kitchen on their computer by trying out different wallpapers, locating cabinets and appliances, mixing colors, and so forth. As a result of this growing emphasis on other products, AutoCAD now accounts for only 70 percent of Autodesk revenues, down from 95 percent when Bartz came aboard in 1992. Her goal is to get it down to 50 percent over the next several years.

A management team is actually strengthened by a downturn, Bartz maintains, echoing Benhamou. "I will submit that you don't know how good your management team is until they've gone through a tough problem," she says. "A good management team will be able to do it in all times and all cycles." Among the steps that Autodesk took during the Release 13 crisis were a hiring freeze and a six-month delay in salary increases. Bartz also spent a lot of time meeting with employees and with customers, working to regain confidence. What Bartz did well was avoiding the impulse to place blame, says Ajay Kela, senior director of software development. "She didn't say Release 13 would bring the company down or fault the programmers. There wasn't a sense of doom."

Steve McMahon, vice president of human resources at Autodesk, says the first reaction to Release 13 was denial. "We just felt that our customers don't understand, they had to be educated about the [product] changes." He says Bartz worked hard to convince people internally and externally of that at first. "Carol was so intent on being successful that she was in a bit of denial, too, for a couple of months. She was trying to support the product people and Release 13." Then realization set in. "We knew we had to get our act together. We had to acknowledge there were problems." At that point, Bartz "started operating more as a healer than a CEO. She had to get the engineering team motivated for Release 14," intended to put the company back on track. Release 13 "was the single biggest mistake we've made," says McMahon. After some intense self-examination and reflection, "we've rebuilt our confidence. Carol shepherded us through a period of feeling pretty crappy and contrite to a period of learning and testing and making it happen for customers."

With the successful introduction of Release 14, Autodesk does appear to be coming out of its trough, which lasted about 18 months. Not all of the effects were bad, Bartz says. "People won't change unless there's a problem," she notes. "When does everybody go on a new diet? When do they stop smoking? When there's a cause for pause. You get hit with some tough issues and companies can change, for the better or the worse." Autodesk changed for the better, she believes. "We learned that we really had to love the customer, and that we had to work together to achieve customer satisfaction." Adds McMahon: "This time last year [late 1996] we were in the penalty box. We paid our dues and now it's beginning to show."

Autodesk's experience demonstrates that even a company with a long history of success can take its eye off the ball and falter. Then, because a big company like Autodesk has more complexity and is accountable to more people than a smaller one, it's much harder for it to reposition itself. The recovery from Release 13 was a long, painful process, but Bartz seems to have pulled it off, which is probably why her name reportedly was on the short list of candidates to head up Silicon Graphics and Apple, both of which face turnaround situations.

■ MICROSOFT PHOBIA

Novell, a once-blooming technology company based in Provo, Utah, subsequently dug itself into a very deep hole and has gone through two CEOs trying to dig itself out. In the early 1980s, Novell pioneered the market for network operating systems, which allow separate computer users to share files. The hero of that story was CEO Ray Noorda, who with the introduction of the NetWare product line in 1983, remade a tiny, struggling hardware manufacturer into the leading network software company. Novell dominated its market segment for nearly a decade, until Microsoft positioned Windows NT as a direct competitor. The aging Noorda became obsessed with beating Microsoft—so much so that a July 1994 *Upside* cover portrayed him as

Captain Ahab hunting the great white whale. Noorda spent nearly $2 billion to buy applications companies that would allow Novell to provide the same range of desktop products as its number one competitor. Focused on a market that Microsoft had already won, Novell missed the shift to the Internet that might have been its salvation.

In 1994 Novell's board ousted Noorda in favor of Bob Frankenberg, a 25-year veteran of Hewlett-Packard. Though Frankenberg shed Noorda's ill-conceived acquisitions, he failed to provide a compelling vision for Novell. Drifting and losing additional market share to Microsoft, the company was in danger of becoming another historical footnote (like Gary Kildall's Digital Research, which Novell had taken over years earlier). In late 1996 Frankenberg resigned under pressure, and Novell launched a search for yet another CEO. Several months later the board picked Eric Schmidt, the chief technology officer of Sun Microsystems as Novell's savior. It was a surprising choice. The bespectacled Schmidt is a computer afficionado who knows technology inside and out, but he had never been renowned for his management abilities. As CTO of Sun, he was best known for his shoot-from-the-hip sound bites, usually aimed at Microsoft.

As chairman and CEO of Novell, Schmidt has faced a much more serious challenge, and many pundits speculated that he might be overmatched. One headline described his job at Novell as "the second-toughest" in high tech (the first is saving Apple). "Being CEO is a serious pain in the ass," jokes Schmidt, who can't quite tame his gunslinger mouth. "You don't have a lot of control over your time and you have all these constituencies to please. But if you haven't been a CEO before, the best kind to be is one in a turnaround. The fastest way to learn is to be in a crisis situation. Every weakness the company has is amplified. You're forced to deal with them." When he joined, Schmidt, who operates out of Novell's second headquarters in San Jose, found the company in "even worse shape than I thought." Instead of being able to focus on developing a new direction, he had to deal with matters like too much unsold inventory piling up in distribution channels, and a plummeting revenue-per-employee figure.

Ron Heinz, senior vice president of worldwide sales for Novell, recalls that with Schmidt, "I had a fear that we were bringing in a technologist who would not be able to grasp business practices." But Heinz was soon impressed with the new CEO's management acumen. "I told Eric we had way too much product in the channel, and he got that very quickly and let me do what needed to be done." In mid-1997, Schmidt approved pulling back $190 million in inventory. Revenue plunged 75 percent, from $365 million in the third quarter of 1996 to a woeful $90 million a year later. Now, says Heinz, "going forward we've got a chance to be successful."

Schmidt also undertook the grim task of cutting 1,000 jobs, almost a fifth of the workforce, in the largest layoff in Novell's history. "You have to do a layoff," he says. "That way they know you're serious. It's like every successful president of the United States has had a war. There's something about that that causes you to become a president, as opposed to a politician." He hastens to add that the layoff was no lighthearted matter. "It changed me and my perception of this job. You're in charge of the livelihoods of 5,000 employees, and we have a lot of Mormons [because of Novell's Utah origins] so they each have about seven mouths to feed per job," he says. "That's 40,000 dependents." When it came time for the layoff, "I had to strap myself to the front of the boat and say, 'We're doing it.' "

Schmidt notes that 46 percent of the vice presidents, 29 percent of the directors, and 18 percent of the rank-and-file employees were terminated. "In the first two months I figured out the lower you were in the organization, the higher the quality of the people," he says. Managers were told to rank their people in terms of their value in going forward with the company. "People who were laid off didn't justify their continued employment here," says Schmidt. "It wasn't fun, and I didn't do it as a learning experience. I did it because we had no choice. Given that, it was an opportunity to establish a new regime that was serious."

For those who were left, "the layoffs were positive," says Michael Simpson, director of marketing for the network services group. "We had an enormous amount of fat left over from the acquisitions. The revenue per employee had dropped from $290,000 to $220,000, and then we ended up getting rid of most of the technology we acquired." The downsizing meant the people who were left "had a sense of urgency," he adds. "Until then, any energy we had was being diluted dramatically by a lack of direction. You start assuming the people above you aren't any smarter than you are, so you wind up making decisions that are ill-informed." Product development cycles ballooned and management would try to fix things at the last moment, forcing even more delays. "It was anarchy," Simpson says.

Though Schmidt so far has shown himself a tougher, more capable executive than anybody expected, Novell has a long way to go. "We need to be smart. We need to be lucky. Maybe Microsoft will stumble," he says wishfully. But he isn't depending on somebody else messing up. "You can manufacture luck to some degree by having fundamental value for the customer." At the minimum, Novell will be "well managed, honest, and ethical. Ultimately, business is built on trust. We may not be as wildly successful as some of these other companies, but our customers will know they can trust us."

Like many of the early technology pioneers, "Novell lucked into a monopoly," Schmidt adds. "They didn't have to sell and they didn't have to be well managed." Schmidt is now managing to outcomes as opposed to process. He explains: "I want people to understand where we want to get to, and to do whatever it takes. I really don't care about people's titles, their promotions, their history. We're in the middle of a turnaround. Whatever petty problem you've got, I am focused on output. If you can't get me there, somebody else will." To further reassure employees, Schmidt boosted the stock options and bonuses for those who are left, and handed out some promotions. "Every employee says, 'Why should I stay here?' I tell them, 'Because if we turn this around, we're all winners.'"

On the technology side, everything Novell does now is related to the Internet that Schmidt also championed at Sun. "We have to be perceived as an Internet leader. We have to ship products that are on the Internet's cutting edge," he says. "That's my commitment." Of course, with a large installed base, Novell will have to be careful to find a way for its customers to move to its next generation of products in an orderly fashion. This so-called migration path was laid out in 1998.

Novell's advantages are that it has plenty of cash, numerous customers who are locked in to NetWare, and a high-energy leader who is also a technology visionary. Schmidt should be able to find any gold hidden in Novell's extensive research and development efforts. Meanwhile, he says, "Microsoft has largely decided it has beaten Novell, so we're below their radar screen." Indeed, Microsoft has been preoccupied with running battles with Sun, Netscape Communications, Oracle, and the U.S. government. "I'm trying to avoid random attacks on Microsoft," says Schmidt. "Our customers are best served by collaboration. Every one of my customers is a Microsoft customer. They're best served by two companies working reasonably well together."

At the end of 1997, Schmidt had some good news to report: In Novell's fiscal fourth quarter ended October 31, 1997, expenses dropped by $26 million and the company reported a small profit of $7.2 million on revenue of $269 million. That was still behind results a year earlier, but it represented a significant improvement over the money-losing second and third quarters. "We're breathing a sigh of relief," Schmidt told the *Wall Street Journal*. Most important, the fourth quarter was a sign that the tenuous turn-around had begun. For 1998 and beyond, Schmidt tells me he would be satisfied to avoid any big negative surprises, get through the Internet transition, and keep revenue and

VIEW FROM THE TOP

Eric Schmidt, CEO, Novell

On Novell:

"Novell needs to be perceived as an Internet leader. We have to ship products that are Internet leading. We will do that. That's my commitment. When you're in the middle of a turnaround it's hard to know what the financial metrics will be. It's more important to focus on getting the right products to the right companies as quickly as possible. I've been very careful to focus on our product lines, key customers, and the messages about what we're doing."

On Being CEO:

"I had a very good job as chief technology officer of Sun. The concept of going to a small start-up and struggling through the financings was not as interesting to me as taking on a role with a high impact and a lot of risk. For me personally this was a career development thing. I've developed a lot of sympathy for [former Apple CEO] Gil Amelio. I can imagine what his life was like on a daily basis. If you haven't been a CEO before, the best kind to be is one in a turnaround. The weaknesses you have will be exploited immediately. The fastest way to learn to be a good CEO is to be in a crisis situation. Every weakness is amplified. You're forced to deal with them."

On Management:

"My whole CTO training was to be an influencer. I was a persuasive and collaborative guy. I was a reasonably good CTO. I hope to be a reasonably good CEO. As CEO I'm judged based on outcomes. The failure of CEOs is not being

(continued)

VIEW FROM THE TOP (Continued)

able to see what they're trying to accomplish. I managed a billion-dollar business at Sun. I eventually figured out in 15 years of being an executive that there's only one thing that matters—you have to be right. It doesn't matter if you're a good manager or charismatic; you just have to be right. It's important to set the stakes, determine the outcome you want. If it's the right one, people will follow and customers will be happy. People are remarkably resilient to bad management and remarkably responsive to brilliant motivational direction. We're going to innovate and win, compete with Microsoft and win. You have to pick your spots and you have to be right."

On 3Com:

"Eric Benhamou is my hero. If I can be half as good I will be ecstatic. He's my age, soft-spoken, very methodical. Cisco has the economics of a Microsoft, and 3Com is its competitor. From day one Cisco had 50 to 70 percent market share. [Cisco CEO John] Chambers is a guy in a hurry. Every meeting I've had with him, he's in a hurry. 3Com has a stabilizing revenue base and is acquiring companies and building a portfolio. Eric had an existing base. He took about two seconds to figure out how to get 80 percent market share in that business. He used the money to cross-subsidize into adjacent markets."

On Acquisitions:

"Once the revenue base is stable you can expect acquisitions. When you have $1 billion in cash everyone expects acquisitions, but the quality of management has to be in place first.

(continued)

VIEW FROM THE TOP (Continued)

On Motivation:

"First you have to make your customers happy—selling them products with the right message. You over-communicate to your employees. Every employee says, 'Why should I stay here?' You communicate with employees every time you do it outside."

On the Future of Novell:

"We need to be lucky. Maybe Microsoft will stumble. You can manufacture luck to some degree, but there has to be fundamental value. You have to see fundamental value, unique talents. If it's a company of 100 percent B players, they will all lose their jobs. The industry is now organized around A players, each of whom dominates their center of excellence."

earnings moving along. "Ultimately, where Novell is five years from now will be defined by how our customers respond to what we've done."

■ THE BOTTOM LINE

Late in 1998, Federal Reserve Chairman Alan Greenspan was pointing to the market drop in August and September as a breather that could provide investors with a much-needed reality check. For technology companies, the challenges that difficult times present can result in a refocused vision, a renewed commitment, a paring down of extraneous elements, and a coming together, which combine to make them stronger as they go forward. Paradoxically, too much good fortune can cause a company to stumble, because it becomes complacent and wedded to an installed customer base—as happened to IBM, Digital Equipment, and many others. The technology industry has produced astonishing growth at dizzying speed, but that kind of success can blind you to the need to switch gears every once in a while.

Even mighty Microsoft at first failed to capitalize on the Internet's potential for interconnecting the electronic world because it was so tied to its successful, near-monopolistic desktop computing business. And Intel, whose CEO Andy Grove preaches the motto "Only the paranoid survive," did not fully anticipate the trend toward sub-$1,000 personal computers and the demand for lower-cost microprocessors to run them. Silicon Graphics fell on hard times when it missed the market shift toward lower-cost desktop computers in the business world, and CEO Ed McCracken was ousted as a result. Mistakes are inevitable in any business arena, especially a fast-growing one; if you're not making any, you're standing still and you're going to get eaten alive. But if you don't recognize those mistakes and correct them as soon as possible, you're dead meat.

So mistakes and downturns are unavoidable; it's what you do about them that matters. The first lesson from the experiences of the technology companies just cited: Admit it when you've got a problem. Seize the initiative. Tell the press, customers, analysts, and employees in your own way. Don't hunker down and hope it blows over; it won't. It'll just get worse. The sooner and more openly you deal with a problem, the better, and part of the fix is open, honest external and internal communications. Technology companies treat their employees like team members, which means letting them know when something's gone wrong.

The second lesson follows from the first: If you have to reduce staff, cut projects, or freeze salaries, warn people that these steps may be coming and then carry them out as quickly as possible. Treat the people who are terminated with respect; give them generous severance pay and outplacement assistance. You may need them again someday, and you certainly need their coworkers and friends who are staying with you. Reward those who are left with additional bonuses and stock options, and get them refocused on the task at hand by giving them incentives to reach their goals.

Autodesk and Novell have shown that you can still keep long-term goals in sight even under the short-term pressure to deal with bad news. Autodesk's Bartz entered a new consumer product niche even as she was revamping the company's lead product line. Novell's Schmidt took a huge hit on quarterly revenue and earnings to fix the company's excess inventory problem. He has also set realistic, achievable targets for the company, and not indulged in the ruinous, grandiose posturing of his predecessor Noorda.

Above all, during difficult times, the chief executive needs to be a visible leader, offering assurances that he or she knows where the company is going and "we'll get through this." Autodesk CEO Carol Bartz has monthly sessions in the company cafeteria called "Come communicate with Carol," in which "anyone can show up and ask anything they want." Says she: "You really have to over-communicate in bad times because that's when they want to hear—what is happening, when is it going to be better?" Only CEOs are really in a position to answer that, and if they can't, the company is in danger of going into a death spiral—watching its best people leave, scaring off customers, losing market share. "That which does not kill us makes us stronger," goes the adage, but it applies only if you've got a leader who's figured out the right direction, and a team willing to follow.

Conclusion

At the End of the Day

If I had to sum up the essence of the technology industry in one word, it would be *speed:* speed to mind share, speed to market, and speed to collaboration. Let's look back to CrossWorlds for an example. Six months after the company launch detailed in Chapter 1, CrossWorlds had its first product ready for shipping. The company had reached GA (general availability) on its processware technology. Not only that, recalls an awed public relations person, but in the interim between the company launch and the product announcement, CrossWorlds' CEO Katrina Garnett delivered a healthy baby boy, named Emerson, and was back at work a week later. At the dinner celebrating the product announcement, Garnett confirmed the company's market position and future goals, and had already lined up endorsements from two early customers who are installing CrossWorlds' technology.

Both companies—Bay Networks, a fellow technology company, and Farmland Industries, a $9.1 billion farmer-owned cooperative—described how CrossWorlds' product seems to be able to offer them technology solutions to their problems. Dick Weaver, regional area manager of Farmlands, says the proof will come when his company gets the entire system up and running, expected in mid-1998. "We're staking a good deal of our company's long-term viability [by] betting that CrossWorlds' product will work for us," he says. "We were leaning toward building it ourselves. What convinced us was the cost of doing that versus CrossWorlds' packaged solution. But buying Cross-Worlds is a higher risk for us, and we do have contingency plans if it doesn't work."

This scenario—a promising new product, a gung-ho company, and eager yet skittish customers—is played out daily in the technology industry. CrossWorlds could be "Everystart-up" and Garnett "EveryCEO," reflective of the optimism and enthusiasm that continually recharge this industry. For all of the millions of dollars that have been invested and the billions of dollars that have been reaped, high tech's future rests with that revved-up, red-eyed pro-grammer in the back room who knows that he or she has written a new bit of code that will solve some previously unsolvable problem in a way that hasn't been thought of before. The entire high-tech infrastructure that I've spent ten chapters describing emerged to facilitate and support just such a momentary burst of creativity.

What do the experiences of technology companies teach the rest of the corporate world? First, you need to look at your company's place in that world differently, as something ephemeral and transitory rather than assured and permanent. That point of view enables you to em-brace change itself as constant and to evolve the qualities required to become an agent of change rather than a vic-tim. This is evolution by design, so you enlist others in the effort, from coworkers to partners, from customers to sup-pliers. You make your company an integral part of a web of relationships, thereby enhancing internal and external growth. You shake off complacency by challenging those within your web to consider what happens when the next paradigm shift occurs.

Does the web pull itself apart—or is it resilient enough to build anew, if necessary? To turn to a literary analogy, it's like teaming up Don Quixote's vision with Huckleberry Finn's practical wit. You have to know when to inspire and when to empower; when to cozy up and when to back away; and above all, when to refine and when to throw out and start over. Even as you're mining your own claim, be ready for the next gold rush, which could occur in an entirely unexpected place. Maybe you can't forecast the location of a new strike, but you can create a company that can move anywhere swiftly and triumphantly.

Appendix

Profiles of Companies Featured in This Book*

Ascend Communications, Inc.
Headquarters: Alameda, California
Founded: 1989
URL: www.ascend.com
CEO: Mory Ejabat, 47
Ownership: Public
1997 Revenues: $1.2 billion

Autodesk, Inc.
Headquarters: San Rafael, California
Founded: 1982
URL: www.autodesk.com
CEO: Carol Bartz, 49
Ownership: Public
1997 Revenues: $617 million for year ended January 31, 1998

---

*Profiles are generally of company status as of early 1998.

Check Point Software Technologies Ltd.
Headquarters: Ramat Gan, Israel, and Redwood City, Calif.
Founded: 1993
URL: www.checkpoint.com
CEO: Gil Shwed (parent), 30, and Deborah Triant (U.S. subsidiary), 48
Ownership: Public
1997 Revenues: $82.9 million

Ciena Corporation
Headquarters: Linthicum, Maryland
Founded: 1994
URL: www.ciena.com
CEO: Patrick Nettles, 54
Ownership: Public
1997 Revenues: $374 million for year ended October 31, 1997

Cisco Systems, Inc.
Headquarters: San Jose, California
Founded: 1984
URL: www.cisco.com
CEO: John Chambers, 48
Ownership: Public
1997 Revenues: $6.4 billion for year ended July 31, 1997

CrossWorlds Software, Inc.
Headquarters: Burlingame, California
Founded: 1996
URL: www.crossworlds.com
CEO: Katrina Garnett, 36
Ownership: Private
1997 Revenues: NA

Firefly Network, Inc. [*]
Headquarters: Cambridge, Massachusetts
Founded: 1995
URL: www.firefly.net
CEO: Nicholas Grouf, 29
Ownership: Private
1997 Revenues: NA

First Virtual Corporation
Headquarters: Santa Clara, California
Founded: 1993
URL: www.fvc.com
CEO: Ralph Ungermann, 55
Ownership: Public
1997 Revenues: $18.8 million

Ipsilon Networks, Inc. [†]
Headquarters: Sunnyvale, California
Founded: 1994
URL: www.ipsilon.com
CEO: Brian NeSmith, 36
Ownership: Private
1997 Revenues: NA

Maxager Technology, Inc.
Headquarters: San Rafael, California
Founded: 1996
URL: www.maxager.com
CEO: Michael Rothschild, 45
Ownership: Private
1997 Revenues: NA

NetNoir, Inc.
Headquarters: San Francisco
Founded: 1995

---

[*] Acquired by Microsoft Corporation in April 1998.

[†] Acquired by Nokia of Finland in December 1997.

URL: www.netnoir.com
CEO: E. David Ellington, 37
Ownership: Private
1997 Revenues: NA

Novell, Inc.
Headquarters: Provo, Utah
Founded: 1983
URL: www.novell.com
CEO: Eric Schmidt, 42
Ownership: Public
1997 Revenues: $1 billion for year ended Oct. 31, 1997

OnLive, Inc.*
Headquarters: Cupertino, California
Founded: 1994
URL: www.onlive.com
CEO: Betsy Pace, 44 (replaced in 1998 by Larry Samuels)
Ownership: Private
1997 Revenues: NA

Open Market, Inc.
Headquarters: Burlington, Massachusetts
Founded: 1994
URL: www.openmarket.com
CEO: Gary Eichhorn, 43
Ownership: Public
1997 Revenues: $61.3 million

PeopleSoft, Inc.
Headquarters: Pleasanton, California
Founded: 1987
URL: www.peoplesoft.com
CEO: Dave Duffield, 57
Ownership: Public
1997 Revenues: $805 million

---

*In early 1998, merged with two other small companies, retaining OnLive name.

Scopus Technology, Inc. *
Headquarters: Emeryville, California
Founded: 1991
URL: www.scopus.com
CEO: Ori Sasson, 36
Ownership: Public
1997 Revenues: $87.6 million

Siebel Systems, Inc.
Headquarters: San Mateo, California
Founded: 1993
URL: www.siebel.com
CEO: Tom Siebel, 45
Ownership: Public
1997 Revenues: $118.8 million

Starwave Corporation †
Headquarters: Bellevue, Washington
Founded: 1993
URL: www.starwave.com
CEO: Mike Slade, 40
Ownership: Private
1997 Revenues: NA

Tenth Planet Explorations, Inc.
Headquarters: Half Moon Bay, California
Founded: 1994
URL: www.tenthplanet.com
CEO: Cheryl Vedoe, 44
Ownership: Private
1997 Revenues: NA

3Com Corporation
Headquarters: Santa Clara, California
Founded: 1979

---

*In March 1998, agreed to be acquired by Siebel Systems.

†Became wholly owned subsidiary of Walt Disney Company in May 1998.

URL: www.3com.com
CEO: Eric Benhamou, 43
Ownership: Public
1997 Revenues: $5.6 billion

VeriFone, Inc.
Headquarters: Redwood City, California
Founded: 1981
URL: www.verifone.com
CEO: Hatim Tyabji, 52
Ownership: Public (part of Hewlett-Packard Company)
1997 Revenues: $600 million

Visigenic Software, Inc. *
Headquarters: San Mateo, California
Founded: 1993
URL: www.visigenic.com
CEO: Roger Sippl, 43
Ownership: Public
1997 Revenues: $17 million for year ended March 31, 1997

Yahoo!, Inc.
Headquarters: Santa Clara, California
Founded: 1994
URL: www.yahoo.com
CEO: Tim Koogle, 46
Ownership: Public
1997 Revenues: $61 million

---

*Acquired by Borland International (now Inprise Corporation) in March 1998.

Appendix

CEO Characteristics*

PILLARS OF LEADERSHIP

Factor	Highly Correlated Scales	Definitions
Visionary Evangelist	Persuasiveness, vision, creativity, risk-taking, assuming responsibility, independence, achievement, formal presentation, strategic planning	Persuades employees to work toward their vision of the future. Creates, sells, and drives the strategy of the organization. Serves as the spokesperson for the organization and demonstrates confidence in its potential for success. Takes charge, pushes for action, and instills a sense of urgency to achieve the organization's goals.
Consensus/ Team Builder	Sensitivity, interpersonal relations, objectivity, subordinate involvement, open-mindedness, flexibility, facilitating teamwork	Develops teamwork, commitment, alignment, and employee motivation by involving, empowering, and creating a positive work environment. Develops loyalty by investing in building relationships with others and by showing interest in employees' needs, growth, and career development. Is open to their ideas, and willing to share power.
Focused Manager	Short-term planning, self-discipline, dependability, organizing work of others, directiveness, results and productivity, thoroughness, monitoring	Provides organization, focus, and clarity of direction to employees. Good administrator. Structured, disciplined, and skilled at setting short-term targets and goals. Good at setting priorities and meeting commitments. Sets up systems and processes. Worries about the details. Monitors results versus plans, and provides the rigor and control necessary to stay on course and correct for deviations from the plan. Gets results.

*All charts in Appendix B are used by permission of Hagberg Consulting Group.

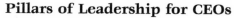

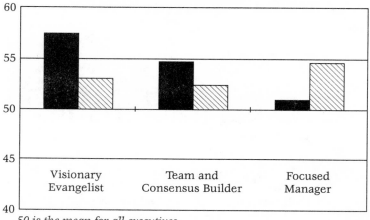

Pillars of Leadership for CEOs

50 is the mean for all executives.

■ Best Large Company CEOs   ▨ Best Small Company CEOs

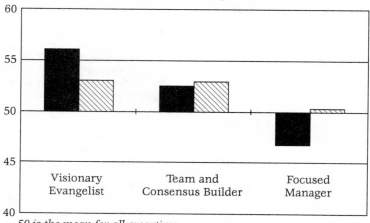

Pillars of Leadership for CEOs

50 is the mean for all executives.

■ Large Company   ▨ Small Company

CEO Self-Rated Personality Scales: Performance Dimensions that *Increase* with Age

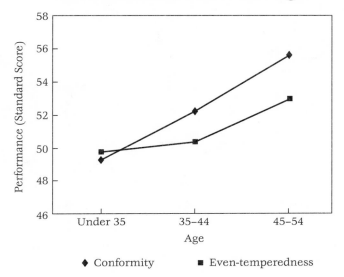

CEO Self-Rated Personality Scales: Performance Dimensions that *Decrease* with Age

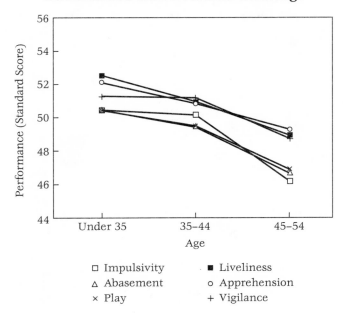

CEO Performance Ratings: Performance Dimensions that *Increase* with Age

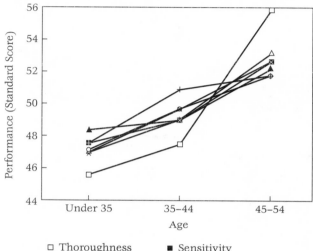

Thoroughness □   ■ Sensitivity
Open-Mindedness △   o Listening
Facilitating ×   + Short-Term Planning
Teamwork   ▲ Subordinate Involvement

Performance Ratings: Performance Dimensions that *Decrease* with Age

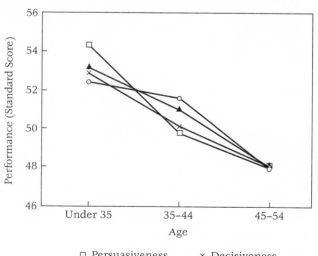

Persuasiveness □   × Decisiveness
Risk Taking ▲   o Creativity

Appendix

Compensation Trends

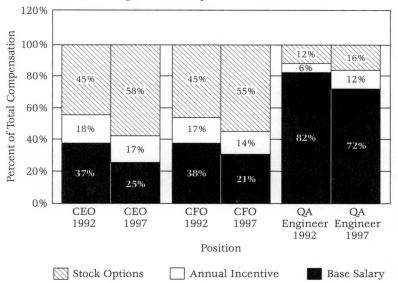

High-Tech Pay Mix Trends

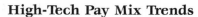

Overall, stock options make up a larger percentage of total compensation in 1997 than 1992. For CEO and CFO positions, the majority of the pay mix is in the form of stock options with annual incentives being the smallest component. For the QA engineer positions, the overwhelming majority of the pay mix remains the base salary component. Though the stock option component increased, it does not play as big a factor in the pay mix as in the CEO and CFO pay mix.

Source: iQuantic client surveys and Radford Associates surveys, used by permission.

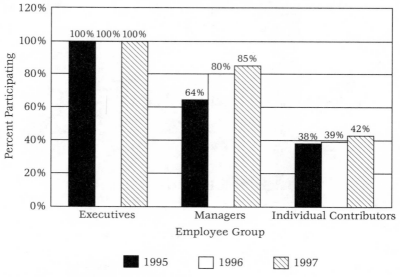

Trends in High-Tech Stock Option Participation, 1995–1997

Source: iQuantic, Inc., used by permission.

1996 High-Technology Stock Option Utilization Rates by 1996 Company Revenue

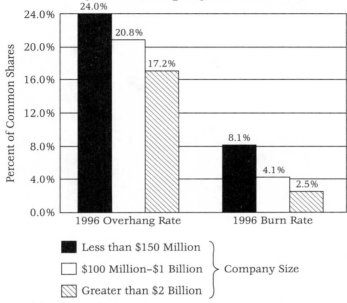

Companies which generated revenue of less than $150 million had the highest overhang and burn rate while companies with the highest revenue, greater than $2 billion, had the lowest overhang and burn rates.

Overhang rate: The total number of outstanding options (vested and unvested) plus the shares reserved for option pool, all divided by the common shares outstanding.

Burn rate: The total number of options granted in a fiscal year divided by the common shares outstanding that year.

Source: iQuantic, Inc., used by permission.

Index